CHÂTEAUX OF THE LOIRE

Contributors:

SIMONE D'HUART
Chief Curator at Archives of France.

MARTINE TISSIER DE MALLERAIS
Curator of Château and Museums of Blois.

JEAN SAINT-BRIS
Curator of Château of Clos-Lucé.

HENRI DE LINARÈS
Curator of International Museum of the Hunt - Gien.

DANIEL OSTER
Institut of France.

MONIQUE JACOB
Curator of Museums in Château of Saumur.

FRANÇOIS BONNEAU
Curator of Château of Valençay.

MAURIZIO MARTINELLI
Art historian.

Photographic service by
GIANNI DAGLI ORTI

BONECHI

© Copyright 1998 by Casa Editrice Bonechi, via Cairoli, 18/b, 50131 Florence, Italy
Phone (055) 576841 - Fax (055) 5000766
E-mail: bonechi@bonechi.it
Internet: www.bonechi.it

Distributed by:
OVET-PARIS
13, rue des Nanettes - 75011 Paris
Phone 43 38 56 80

Photo p. 87 bottom: Daniel and Emmanuelle Minassian (courtesy of the Château de Langeais)

Map: Studio Grafico Daniela Mariani, Pistoia

Printed in Italy by Centro Stampa Editoriale Bonechi.

ISBN 88-7009-380-8

* * *

INTRODUCTION

It seems natural to wonder why so many châteaux are situated along a river and its tributaries on a patch of land 200 kilometers long and 100 wide.

The reason may lie partly in the clear blue skies and peaceful valley of a river that runs through the heart of France, far from troubled frontiers.

On the other hand the fact that the Hundred Years' War (1337-1453), in which the idea of a nation came to the fore, was resolved here, on the river, cannot be overlooked.

Each and every one of these reasons is involved but the single most valid reason is that when the members of the house of Valois returned from the wars in Italy (begun in 1494) their ideas of "residence" and "court" were no longer the same.

Their castles, which up to then had been little more than rude strongholds, had lost their raison d'être, for peace at home was now ensured and the invention of artillery had turned walls that seemed impregnable into fragile screens.

Charles VIII, Louis XII and Francis I had assimilated the Italian model in which the measure of royal power was no longer armed might but culture, elegance, ostentation, a daily life immersed in luxury and a love of the spectacular and of being seen.

Louis XII had called Laurana and Niccolò Spinelli from Italy and had left the palace of the Louvre for Plessis-les-Tours. This is how it all began. Italian culture had made a breach.

When Charles VIII returned from Naples in 1495, Italian artists followed in his wake. The old strongholds began to be opened up, the walls were emptied and light was finally allowed to enter.

Only a few characteristic elements of the castle-fortress still remained: the machicolations, for example, were transformed into ornamental motifs (Amboise, Chaumont, Chenonceaux, Azay-le-Rideau, Chambord). Openings were surrounded by friezes, and chimneys made their appearance on the roofs as real sculptural elements.

Landscape gardening, with its fountains, ornamental waterworks, hedges alternated with flower-beds, was created as an art together with the art of living. Among the artists who accompanied Charles VIII when he returned from Italy was Fra' Pacello da Marcogliano, the inventor of open spaces, who had been carried away from the Court of Naples and who had never forgotten the precise green geometrical patterns of the Sicilian orange groves.

When he was in Naples Charles VIII had lived in Poggioreale which was more like a stage set for fêtes and periods of relaxation than a castle. When he returned to France, he transformed the old fortress of Amboise into a series of halls, gardens, terraces, galleries.

Charles d'Amboise, sent to Milan by order of his king, Louis XII, returned overcome by the splendid life at court and the pomp and ceremony of the Visconti court and he, too, transformed his castle of Meillant.

This was when the Loire acquired a central role in the arts. The flamboyant style of the châteaux is a new dimension in the art of the court.

The nobility and the new wealth of the bourgeoisie gravitated around the Court. Bankers and financiers such as Berthelot at Azay-le-Rideau, Bohier at Chenonceaux, were so powerful that the kings graciously accepted loans from them.

And there were also merchants like Jacques Coeur, whose ships and whose storehouses overflowing with silks, cotton, spices and products of the

Orient can still today be admired in the stained-glass windows in Bourges.

And there was also Salviati, the Italian banker, whose chief merit in addition to making loans to nobles and kings, is that of having had a daughter, Cassandra, who served as inspiration for Ronsard, the greatest Renaissance poet in French literature. Peace at home and the absence of tensions along the borders permitted the kings to carry on a policy of prestige and splendor which was externalized in the lacy pile of stone which is Chambord, and which, like Versailles later on, was meant to dazzle Europe. Even the ambassador of the Serenissima was left breathless - and he came from Venice. And the nobles sought to emulate the life style of the king.

The Amboise family built Chaumont; the house of Hurault, Cheverny.

The cities began to be built in the style which still survives in their historical centers: Tours, Blois, Angers, Orleans, cities that seem to have been carved, not built.

It was pure chance that on May 29, 1418, the history of the Loire as a royal residence began with the flight of the dauphin of France (the future Charles VII) who sought refuge in Bourges from the Burgundian hordes. Had they wanted to, the kings who succeeded him could have returned to live in Paris once it had been reconquered.

Instead they chose to live on the banks of the river. And thus for 170 years, one of the most resplendent periods in the history of France unravelled along the valley of the Loire.

The river was a vital waterway along which the square sails of the boats and barges slowly moved.

It was the natural way to the sea which it meets at Nantes. Silks, spices, pearls, precious stones, works of art, war trophies all arrived via the river.

Charles VIII had his Italian booty brought up the river: one hundred and thirty tapestries, 39 leather wall panels with scenes in gold, lengths of velvet and damasks, illuminated books, paintings and sculpture. The booty was accompanied by tailors, cabinet-makers, makers of organs, decorators, a maker of artificial incubators and even a parrot breeder.

The river too, and a project for the canal of Amboise, is how Francis I convinced Leonardo, who was already old, to follow him to France with "La Gioconda", which he bought for 4,000 ducats. The grand old man lived in Clos-Lucé, in the residence prepared for him, in close touch with the king. Here he received frequent visits, the honor and the respect his fame inspired.

Besides canals, Leonardo designed automata which frightened the court ladies, fireworks and great public illuminations which concluded the days spent hunting in Amboise and Chambord.

The guests were ambassadors, important dignitaries and sovereigns. Among these was the Emperor Charles V, who considered the castle as a "summus" of human ingenuity.

A glimpse of court life in the 16th century may also be useful in understanding the period.

In 1539 when Charles V, emperor of Spain and Flanders, arrived in Chambord the whole valley was in ferment.

Fêtes of all kinds, perhaps the most sumptuous ever planned, were in preparation.

Long rows of wagons, servants unloading enormous quantities of food: oysters and fish from the Atlantic, huge trophies of fruit, plumed wildfowl, quarters of deer, barrels of wine. Tables set with silver, roaring fires.

Walls lined with fabrics, the perfume of incense, lutes, guitars, torches held by pages, with light flickering on the fresh complexions and jewels of the ladies.

In the procession the king and the queen, young princesses and princes of Europe, the dauphin Henry II and his young wife Catherine de' Medici who learned the lesson well and later organized ceremonies that were grander and more ruinous.

The fêtes, the balls, the tournaments, were the culminating moment in the life of a court that also lived on intrigue: stories of repudiated wives, of ill-assorted marriages, of murders, courtesans and secret struggles for power. All set against the backdrop of the châteaux which become more and more beautiful.

Every residence, be it royal, noble, or bourgeois, has its stories of hidden life which will be discovered in the pages that follow. From the murder of the Duke de Guise to the perfidious play of jealousy between the great Catherine de' Medici and the equally powerful courtesan Diane de Poitiers, to whom Henry II had given, as a gift, one of the less spectacular but more amenable châteaux, Chenonceaux, which at the death of the king once more returned into the hands of the queen.

She installed herself in the castle with her "Escadron Volant" consisting of the youngest and loveliest ladies of France whose role was that of entertaining the palace guests.

The fêtes were no longer the fabulous and regal spectacles they once had been but now were a matter of play: disguises, verdant hiding places, a switching of roles.

Extravagances in which the lovely ladies of the "Escadron Volant" dressed (or undressed) as available Nymphs (as described by Brantôme) served sumptuous banquets in the shade of rockworks. Catherine's decadence and refinement was handed down and accentuated in the three kings she bore to Henry II -Francis II, Charles IX and above all Henry III, the most frivolous and immoral of the lot, who alternated between mystical crises and the most licentious entertainment which cost the treasury a fortune and his subjects exorbitant crushing taxes.

Then came the religious wars, the night of St. Bartholomew (August 24, 1572), the plague which appeared more than once - in 1583, in 1584 and in 1586. In 1607 it decimated the population of Tours.

Dearth and famine followed.

The fortunes of the nobles and the greater bourgeoisie melted away in their attempts to imitate the ostentation of the Court. The valley was impoverished. The important silk industries languished, agriculture was degraded.

The decline of the valley coincided with the end of the house of Valois. The regal processions which wound their way through the valley from fêtes and entertainment in one dwelling to those in another kept on dwindling.

Palaces that were large, and stable, and monumental began to be appreciated.

The star of Fontainebleau waxed brighter.

The châteaux of the Loire had reached the end of their roles as leading actors, and they now stand as extraordinary witnesses of times gone by and gems of a glorious epoch.

Elsa Nofri Rosi

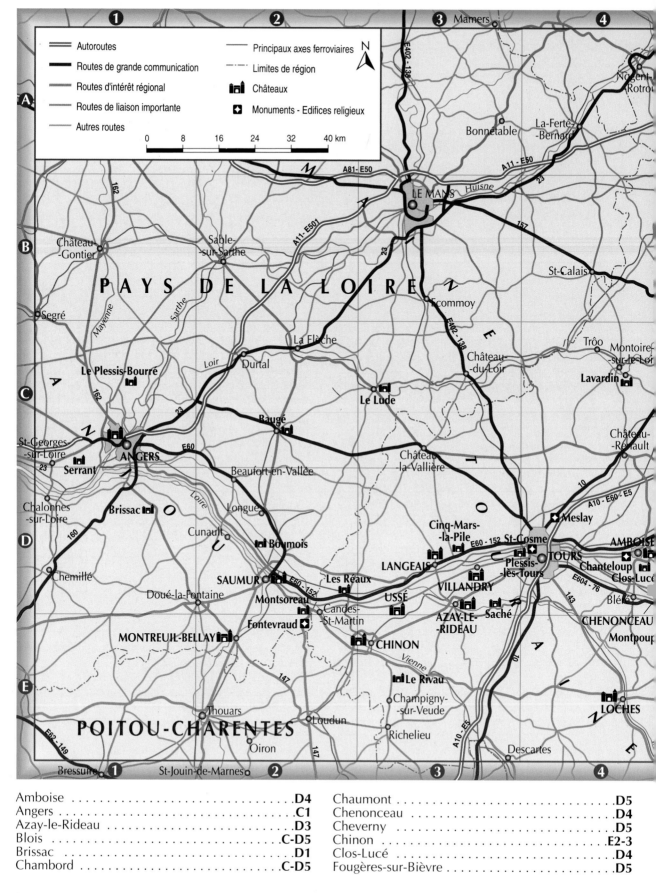

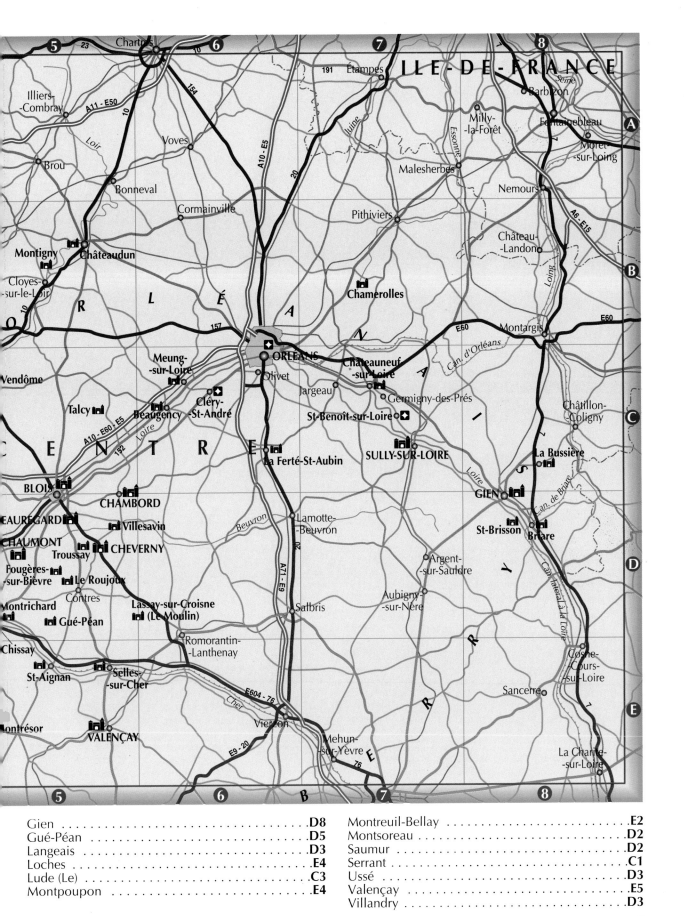

The castle seen from the river.

AMBOISE

Amboise first appeared in history around 503 when Clovis I, king of the Franks, and Alaric II, king of the Visigoths, met on the Île St-Jean, in the center of the Loire, below the present castle.

Devastated by the Normans more than once, Amboise was first part of the possessions of the counts of Anjou and then belonged to the famous house of Amboise-Chaumont until 1422 when it was inherited by Louis, viscomte of Thouars. Found guilty of plotting against the king, the owner of the château of Amboise was deprived of his lands.

From 1431 on, the castle belonged to the Crown. The "chastel d'Amboise" was no longer solely a fortress, but a royal residence and the city was benefited by the concession of receiving payment of the franchise. The children of King Louis XI and Charlotte of Savoy were born here and Amboise became the residence of the queen and her children, while the sovereign preferred to keep his court at Plessis-les-Tours.

One of the great events in his reign was the creation at Amboise of the Order of Saint Michael on the first of August in 1469. That day the king gathered together fifteen of his most powerful barons in the chapel of St. Michael to acquaint them with the statute of this order of knighthood, whose foundation was of specifically political significance. The order of Saint Michael represented the bond that tied the great lords and landed proprieters to the royal Crown.

Luxuriously robed in long damask cloaks embroidered with golden shells and lined with ermine, their heads covered with crimson velvet headdresses with long cornettes, these great lords swore to live according to the laws of the Church and Knighthood. That day Amboise was the scene of a grand ceremony which remained in the annals of the kingdom.

The queen, who died there in 1483, was always surrounded by a large court as befitted her rank. She had almost 150 persons in her following and service. The apartments had been decorated and furnished in an effort to make her abode as pleasing as possible.

The serene life he had lived there when he was young explains why the new King Charles VIII was so attached to the château where he had been born and raised. It was in the Place du Carroir at Amboise that the young 13-year old dauphin received Margaret of Austria, granddaughter of Charles the Bold, whom his father had decided to give him as wife. Margaret was only three years old when she was engaged to Charles VIII and lived in the château of Amboise until 1492 when she had to return to Flanders with a heavy heart, ceding her post to Anne de Bretagne whom Charles VIII had married on December 6, 1491. Great construction works were undertaken at this time, financed by the income from the taxes. The plans were magnificent: "he wants to turn the castle into a city" exclaimed the Florentine ambassador when he saw the projects late in 1493. The area of the building had to be considerably enlarged. A large trapezoid divided into three courtyards took the place of the old medieval fortress, with the main courtyard for the king's dwelling, the "logis des Vertus" to the south, and lastly the courtyard known as "cour du donjon", at the western extremity of the promontory.

The two spiral turrets, the Minimes tower and the Hurtault tower, were important architectural innovations. As for the decoration, it was initially of French inspiration but later profitted from the collaboration of Flemish artists and, after the return of the Italian expedition of 1495, of Italian artists. The furnishings were luxurious: Flemish and French tapestries, Damask curtains and Turkish carpets.

The imposing construction works which aimed at transforming the antique "oppidum" and the old fortress of the counts of Anjou into an abode worthy of the Crown of France were interrupted by a mortal accident that befell the king in Amboise on April 7, 1498. While Charles was accompanying the queen in the Haquelebac gallery on his way to a ball game, it is said, he hit his forehead on a low door and died a few hours later. What kind of future was now in store for Amboise, left without the king who had been born there and who had died there at the age of 28?

His successor was the duke of Orléans who took the name of Louis XII, but the château of his choice was Blois where much work was done during his reign and where he went to live with Anne de Bretagne, widow of Charles VIII, whom he married on January 8, 1499.

In 1500-1501 work was renewed and great quantities of stone were brought in to complete the buildings, particularly the Hurtault tower, and to create the gardens on the terraces above the Loire. With the accession of Francis I the château once more shone. From 1515 to 1518 the king sojourned in what he called "that sumptuous château" when he came to the banks of the Loire, and after Marignano he returned to Amboise in 1516. Queen Claude gave birth to her three children here.

Amboise was at the center of European politics, for the great treaties which marked the beginning of his reign were signed here: the peace of Noyon with the king of Spain, the Concordat with Pope Leo X, perpetual peace with the Swiss, the treaty of Cambrai with the Emperor and the treaty of London with Henry VIII. This was also where Francis had prepared his candidacy to the imperial throne receiving the most important personages in Germany.

Under Henry II's reign, Catherine de' Medici, who loved Amboise, lived there with the children of the royal house. The château was later abandoned by the court of Valois and if the young King Francis II and his wife Mary Stuart, the queen mother, children, servants and following all arrived there on February 22, 1560 at

View of the royal apartments from the garden.

Following pages: the hall of the States General, Henry II's bedroom and the capel of St. Hubert. ▶

Exterior of the chapel of St. Hubert.

Interior of the chapel with Leonardo da Vinci's tomb.

the beginning of the new regime this was because they had to flee from Blois and the conspiracy plotted by Condé which broke out at the beginning of the month.

The famous conspiracy of Amboise was severely repressed and three years later, on May 19, 1563, the queen mother, Catherine de' Medici, and the Prince de Condé stipulated the treaty which put an end to the first religious uprisings and allowed freedom of worship to the Protestant aristocracy.

After these extraordinary events the château of Amboise ceased to be a royal residence even though Louis XIII lived there off and on. In 1627 it became part of the property of Gaston d'Orléans and in 1660 returned to the Crown of France.

But at that time the château was no longer really liveable for it had in part been demolished. In 1762 the duke of Choiseul bought the château, the baronage and the territory of Amboise which his heirs sold in 1786 to the duke of Penthièvre. This prince, a relative of Louis XIV, was the most wealthy lord of his time and owned more than twenty châteaux and palaces. In the years which preceded the Revolution he ordered work, including new construction, to be done in the building which was at the center of the duchy from 1787 on. During the Revolution the château was confiscated and once more despoiled. Army barracks were installed and a button factory was set up between the logis des Sept-Vertus and the chapel of Saint Hubert.

But it was only later, under the First Empire, that Amboise was most seriously mutilated and even systematically demolished by the member of parliament Roger-Ducos, who as senator was a beneficiary of the settlement of Orleans and was assigned the château of Amboise as his residence. Lacking the means to maintain it, the only solution he found was that of largely destroying it. In 1815 it was restored to the heiress, the duchess of Orleans.

When the duchess of Orleans died in 1821, her son, the future King Louis Philippe, inherited the château and the property of Amboise. Louis Philippe acquired 46 houses and barracks which surrounded the château in rue des Minimes and at Porte Hurtault and had them torn down, freeing the towers and the encircling walls as well as providing access to the cellars which stretched out under the château and its "dependances", particularly those which are still called the "ancient granaries of plenty of Julius Caesar".

From 1848 to 1852 the château of Amboise had an unexpected guest, the Arabian emir, Abd-el-Kader, who spent four years here until Napoleon III, prince-president, personally came to Amboise on October 16, 1852, to communicate his newly acquired liberty.

In 1974, when it was created, the Saint-Louis Foundation took over the administration of the château and now continues to carry out the restoration which was begun at the end of the last war.

The sturdy towers of the castle of Angers.

ANGERS

Situated on the shores of the Maine river, Angers was once inhabited by fierce Celtic peoples who tenaciously opposed Roman penetration.

After the period of the Norman invasions (9th century) Fulk Nerra, comte d'Anjou, had a castle built here. This first stronghold was replaced by a better furnished architectural complex built by Louis IX, known as St. Louis, between 1228 and 1238, which was then further enlarged by Louis I of Anjou and under Louis II of Anjou, who had the Gothic chapel built.

The court of René of Anjou, known as the Good, regent of Sicily and Jerusalem, resided here. A man of letters and benefactor of the local community, he was fond of fêtes and tournaments which were often held at the castle. In an illuminated manuscript which he himself executed, René illustrated in words and images the pomp that accompanied the tournaments in the castle of Angers, where there were also aviaries and menageries with exotic animals.

The religious wars later led to the decline of the castle and Henry III ordered it to be demolished in 1585. The cylindrical towers of the pentagonal stronghold began to be torn down and the conical roof and the upper part were dismantled. When Henry IV came to the throne the destruction came to a halt and Angers was the scene of the engagement of César of Vendôme with Françoise of Lorraine.

The series of Apocalypse Tapestries, commissioned by Louis I, duke of Anjou, in 1373, is now on exhibit inside the castle. This magnificent textile was originally 140 meters long and is based on cartoons by the painter Jean de Bandol, also called Hennequin de Bruges, and was woven by Nicolas Bataille. The series of panels which illustrate the Book of Revelations of St. John was in the archbishopric of Arles in 1400 and after 1474 in the church of St. Maurice in Angers. In 1782 the tapestries disappeared, to be recovered in 1848 by a canon, Joubert, who had them restored. Each panel is accompanied by the figure of St. John, who participates in and illustrates the scene. The original captions were removed during the 19th-century restoration because of their poor state of preservation.

John's story is difficult to understand and full of allegories whose meaning is not always clear. In the tapestries this occult meaning is respected. In the still extant panels the story begins with John, upon divine invitation, describing his visions for the good of the seven churches, shown as chapels. The symbolism present in this scene pervades the entire work, as is noted in the following panels in which John sees the Messiah, with specific attributes, amidst figures which allegorically represent the accomplishments of Creation. After a scene of homage to the Messiah, comes the lamentation of the saint and the beginning

On these and the following two pages: two views of the hall with the Tapestries of the Apocalypse; St. John, the Angel and the New Jerusalem, represented as a fortified castle; the old man with the long white beard portrays, apart from St. John, the seven churches and also Duke Louis I of Anjou; two tapestries that illustrate the following verses from St. John's Apocalypse: «And the number of soldiers mounted on horseback was 200 million... their armourplating was flame, sapphire- and sulphur-coloured; the horses' heads were like lions' heads»; «... An enormous flame-coloured dragone with seven heads and ten horns ... then war broke out in the sky / St. Michael and his angels, on the other side the dragon and his angels».

of the explanation of the divine secrets after the exhibition of the divine lamb. The four riders of the Apocalypse, on different colored horses, are revealed, and after them comes the salvation of the souls of the dead in the service of God. After the identification of the chosen people, new secrets are introduced in the presence of God and an angel. The forces of nature demonstrate their might, unleashed by the first four peals of the divine trumpets in the panels of the storm, the star of fire and the eagle. At the fifth and sixth peals the disorder in the universe increases. In the panels that follow, the mysterious words of the seven claps of thunder are revealed to St. John and he symbolically devours the book of the angel. After John's appraisal of the celestial harmony (with the measuring of the temple) come four panels which narrate the adventure of the two witnesses saved by God and the announcement of the imminent arrival of the Messiah and the Last Judgement. This is followed by the chapter in which Satan, in different forms, persecutes Creation, first as a dragon, attacking a woman in labor who is defended by St. Michael, and battling with the faithful, then as an idolatrous marine monster, and finally as a land monster. After these scenes, angels announce the New Testament, the fall of Babylon and the sufferings of the damned. Then, after the just have been saved they are received by God, while the infidels face divine wrath (which symbolically reaps them like grapes at harvest time). The representation of the seven scourges which accompany the wrath of God is followed by the appearance of three satanic beasts and the whore of Babylon, mother of abominations, who finally fall, together with the defeat of the three beasts and Satan himself. The series of tapestries ends with the image of the celestial Jerusalem, the city of which St. John measures the perfection and finally prostrates himself before the Trinity.

The castle at sunset.

AZAY-LE-RIDEAU

The château of Azay-le-Rideau is situated on an enchanting bend of the Indre river. Most probably the name Azay derives from the Latin Asiacus, the name of the owner of these lands, and the village of Azay dates back to Roman times. In the Middle Ages, thanks to the presence of a small fortress, it stood watch over the local ford over the Indre.

In the 12th century the owner was Rideau or Ridel d'Azay, whose fierceness earned him the nickname "Child of the Devil". Henry II Plantagenet expropriated all his lands, but they were later restored, together with the castle, by Philip Augustus to Rideau's son, Hugues, knight of Turenne, who served the king faithfully in the battle of Bouvines. Later, in the early 15th century, the castle seems to have been in the hands of the duke of Burgundy. When the duke offended the dauphin Charles (future Charles VII) and his army, a military attack was launched against the stronghold in 1418: the garrison composed of 354 persons was wiped out and the castle and the nearby town were burned down and completely destroyed. After the fire, which left only ruins in its wake, the place was for a time known as Azay-le-Brûlé. The present château was built a century later on the area of the precedent construction.

A historical panorama of the late 15th century helps to explain the characteristics of the new building. At that time Charles VIII and Louis XII organized military expeditions to Italy where they were impressed by the art and architecture they found there. As a result many artists and craftsmen were called to France in the employ of the king and his followers.

Their mark is most clearly to be seen in the region of the Loire where the royal court resided from the time of Charles VII on. The Italianate style of the châteaux of Amboise and of the remodelling of the castle of Blois was soon copied in the residences of the old noble families and in those of the aspirant nobility. Gilles Berthelot, the owner of a part of the territory of Azay-le-Rideau at the beginning of the 16th century, was just such a man, an important financier whose father, Martin Berthelot, had been Maître de la Chambre des Finances for Louis XI and Charles VIII.

Gilles, in a brilliant career, became a counselor to the King, Maître de la Chambre des Comptes and mayor of Tours. Thanks to his marriage with Philippa Lesbahy, who owned the rest of the territory of Azay, he was able to reunite the entire estate under one owner and begin the grandiose construction of the castle.

With the financial and political backing of various relatives who held important posts, Gilles Berthelot began the reconstruction of the medieval manor in

The ballroom with the Flemish tapestries.

The dining-room with its Henry II style furniture.

1518. That summer, under the supervision of the master builder Etienne Rousseau, as many as 120 laborers were at work preparing the foundations. What was left of the previous stronghold had to be eliminated and the area then had to be drained before setting up the wooden pilings on which the whole building rests. Cream-colored tuff from the Cher valley was used for the building itself. The blocks were carried on barges as far as Port-aux-Chalands near Vallères and then the stones were transported on wagons for the remaining ten kilometers.

The château has an unusual L-shaped ground plan and its architectural details reveal the evolution from the Gothic to the Renaissance style and a new concept of the dwelling which is no longer a stronghold but a pleasant residence. Only an occasional element of military architecture, lightened by a Renaissance imprint, remains side by side with a few aspects that are still Gothic, like the high-pitched slate roofs. This was due as much to the taste of Philippa, who kept close track of the proceedings and supervised the construction work, conferring an exquisitely feminine touch to the building, as it was to the work of the master builder Rousseau, the sculptor Pierre Maupoint and the carpenter Jacques Thoreau. Balzac, who wrote "Le Lis dans la Vallée" near Azay, described the château in

The bedroom of Pierre Filley de la Barre.

A detail of the embroidery on the silk bedspread. ▶

these words: "coming to the top of the hill I admired for the first time this faceted diamond, inserted in the Indre, mounted on pilasters decorated with flowers".

Seen from the outside the castle has angle towers set on walls which jut out from the main building and which are linked together on the outside by a sentinel walk. This was built out of respect for the preceding tradition and has no function at all in a castle without an enclosed courtyard. Numerous references to the Italian Renaissance are to be found side by side with elements which imitate the dwellings of the older French nobility. The pilasters with their capitals which support the horizontal cornices, the superstructures of the dormer windows with pediments, volutes and shell-shaped clouds, and the overall symmetry reveal an Italianate classicizing inspiration. This is also the case of the staircase of honor, entrance to which is through twin doors surmounted by reliefs of Francis I's salamander and the ermine of Claude de France. The three upper levels of the staircase are characterized by straight flights with landings which lead to the two-light Italianate loggias which overlook the garden below. The ceilings over the stairs have stone coffering

bordered by arches in which the portraits of the 15th- and 16th-century kings and queens were sculptured in the 19th century. The innovation of this staircase makes it one of the key points of French Renaissance architecture - under the stimulus of new concepts the narrow spiral staircase of medieval origin was abandoned. Broad straight flights of stairs became popular, no longer illuminated by narrow louvers but by large loggias which provide a view over the park as well as letting in light. There are various rooms inside the château on the ground floor (the royal room and the red room) as well as more generic rooms and a kitchen. The first floor contains a dining room, a ball room, and a blue room as well as those of Francis I and of Claude de France.

Gilles Berthelot never finished the construction work on the castle. His cousin Semplancay, who was Superintendent of Finances, was accused of having stolen public funds, found guilty, and hanged in Mont-faucon. Gilles found himself in a difficult situation and thought it wise to flee while there was still time. In 1527 he sought refuge in the free city of Metz where he died in exile ten years later. The castle, with all its lands,

The Renaissance bedroom of Francis I.

Detail of the fireplace with the salamander in the bedroom of Francis I.

was confiscated by Francis I who gave it to the captain of the guards, Antoine Raffin, who carried the work to completion.

Later, when the royal seat was definitively removed to Paris by Francis I, Touraine's importance diminished. The château of Azay-le-Rideau belonged to the families of Cossé de Gonnord, Saint Gelais de Lusignan, Vassé. In 1603 a chapel was added, in which the owners of the castle were subsequently buried. In the 17th century the kings of France only rarely sojourned at Azay. In 1619 the Saint Gelais family offered hospitality to Louis XII, while Louis XIV probably sojourned there in 1650. After the building of the annexes at the end of the 17th century (to be used as stables and as servants' quarters), further work was undertaken in 1845 by the Marquis of Biencourt, owner of the château. It was in that year that the right tower of the court of honor, which up till then had still been in the older medieval style, was rebuilt. Twenty years later a second projecting tower was erected in the same style and with the same materials, so as to make one of the facades more symmetrical.

In 1871, after the defeat of the French army, Prussian troops were quartered in the castle which had been requisitioned from the fourth marquis of Biencourt. In that year on the 19th of February Prince Frederick

Charles of Prussia with his general staff was housed there. The tale goes that during supper, which was eaten in the kitchen, a heavy chandelier fell from the keystone in the ceiling onto the prince's table and almost killed him. Frederick thought it was an attempt on his life and the officers had a hard time persuading him not to set fire to the castle in retaliation.

The building later once more became the property of the marchises of Biencourt who sold it in 1904 when the society they administered went bankrupt. The new owner, M. Arteau, sold the château to the State for the sum of 200,000 francs. The building has since been restored while the park and the bend of the Indre again look as they originally did. The rooms inside have been turned into a Renaissance Museum thanks to the recovery of furniture, tapestries, objects of daily use and paintings. Among the material exhibited mention should be made of the tester bed which belonged to the king's marshal, Pierre de Filley de la Barre, who died in the siege of Nice in 1705. This piece of furniture, marked by an animated floral decoration in silk, is in the blue room, while another tester bed with damask, originally in the castle of Effiat, is in the red room. Other pieces of Renaissance furniture in wood furnish the rooms of the castle: the chest in Francis I's room is decorated with small pilasters and with fantastic animals on either side of the two medallions, while in the kitchen is an elegant chest with two profiles carved on the frontal. The kitchen also contains examples of cupboards and utensils in ceramics and in metal, such as grills, fire tongs, forks, basins and pitchers. The collection of tapestries in Azay-le-Rideau includes the 16th-century tapestry of the Three Fates, executed in Brussels, which is on exhibit in the ball room near another tapestry of the same period with plant motifs. On the other walls of this room are four large 17th-century tapestries of Flemish production with biblical scenes such as the Reconciliation of Esau and Jacob, the Judgement of Solomon, the Ark of the Covenant, and the Visit of the Queen of Sheba to Solomon. In the dining room on the ground floor are 16th-century Flemish tapestries with the queen Semiramis, the messenger of the King and Balthazar's feast. The tapestries in the royal chamber, designed by Simon Vouet, represent the love story of Rinaldo and Armida. The two tapestries with the palaces of Vincennes and Versailles in the blue room come from the manufacture of Lille, while those with hunting scenes come from Beauvais. To make the museum more complete these rooms also contain numerous paintings with the portraits of the kings of France and members of the royal family, including Francis I, Henry II, Catherine de' Medici, Francis II, Charles IX, Henry III, Margaret of Valois and Louis XIV.

Detail of a XVIth century trousseau chest.

View of the kitchen.

*H.J. van Blarenberghe (1741-1812) - Water-colour of Blois
at the end of the XVIIIth century.*

BLOIS

Several thousands of years ago the exceptional lie of the land around Blois was noted - a rocky promontory, hollowed out by the junction of the Loire and by a stream, easy to isolate and defend. It was no doubt used as early as the Neolithic Age, even though the existence of the castle was not documented until the 9th century.

Towards the middle of the 10th century, Blois and the surrounding countryside were given in fief to very powerful noblemen, the counts of Blois, vassals of the King of France and also counts of Tours, Chartres and later of Champagne: they rebuilt the fortified castle several times. The only remaining evidence of the imposing fortress built during the 13th century are a corner tower, fragments of ramparts and towers incorporated here and there in later constructions and above all, the large assembly room and ballroom of the counts of Blois.

At the end of the 14th century, the county of Blois was sold to Prince Louis of Orleans, son of the king of France Charles V, initiating a brilliant future for the town. His son, the poet Charles of Orleans, lived in the castle 25 years on his return from serving a long prison sentence in England, attracting a small court of scholars and poets around him. But of even greater importance for the town, his grandson became king of France in 1498 under the name of Louis XII, following on the accidental death in Amboise of his cousin, the young Charles VIII, who died leaving no heirs. Born in Blois, Louis XII decided to fix his residence there. In this way, the small town of Blois became the royal town and capital of the kingdom during part of the 16th century. It was a very fortunate choice as the town and region were rapidly expanding at the time and all their inhabitants were devoted to the dukes of Orleans who had brought them so much prosperity.

At the time of Charles of Orleans, and specially under Louis XII and Francis I, the town of Blois grew considerably. But after the death of Queen Claude de France in 1524 and the disaster of Pavia in 1525, Francis I never returned to Blois and his successors only paid short visits to the town.

During the 17th century, the city was brought back to life by the prolonged stay (1634-1660) of Gaston d'Orleans, brother of Louis XIII.

The kings paid little attention to the château of Blois throughout the 18th century. It was divided into small apartments and used to house old servants of the

The equestrian statue of Louis XII in flamboyant Gothic style.

Francis I's wing seen from the inner courtyard with the famous staircase.

Crown. The gardens were parcelled out and it fell into a state of general neglect. In 1788, Louis XVI ordered the sale of the castle or failing that, its demolition. It was saved by its transformation into a military barracks.

During and after the Revolution, various monuments of Blois were mutilated, or even destroyed stone by stone. The castle did not escape these acts of vandalism and all the emblems and effigies of the royal family were effaced. During the first half of the 19th century, the castle was modified due to its military occupation. In 1845 the architect Duban began a radical restoration of the château which is now considered to have been excessive.

Louis XII wing. In 1948, Louis duke of Orleans and count of Blois became king of France under the name of Louis XII. The new king soon undertook to rebuild his ancestors' castle. The Louis XII wing, which originally extended on three sides of the court, was built rapidly in the space of three years. The new appearance of this gracious manor built in brick and stone is surprising. It is devoid of towers and battlements which were still widespread during that period and the large windows, balconies, skylights and open galleries let in

a great deal of air and light. The architecture of Louis XII's wing is serene, gay and gracious in keeping with a king who was known for his simple, affable manner. It was no longer a fortified castle because Louis XII did not need to defend himself; his power was undisputed. By that stage, the king of France required a castle of government which could be used for receptions and balls. The king introduced a new way of governing, an "open" diplomacy, inspired by the Italians as can be seen from the revolutionary diplomatic act that constitutes the sumptuous reception held in 1501 in the castle of Blois in honour of the Archduke of Austria with whom France was practically at war.

If Louis XII's constructions were modern in design, they remained basically Gothic in many aspects: lack of regularity and symmetry in their plan and distribution of openings; fine, sharp-pointed, hollowed-out mouldings and rich, sculptured decorations, consisting, as in the cathedrals, of friezes of foliage, pinnacles and rosettes and in particular, of corbels with picturesque personages in a very Medieval vein.

According to French and Gothic tradition, the initials and emblems of the owners of the place are sculptured in the stone: fleur-de-lis for the king and

The wing of Gaston d'Orléans, attributed to Mansart.

The Guardroom with its monumental fireplace. ▶

Detail of the salamander and of the ermine ▶
sculptured on the fireplace.

ermine spots for the queen, Anne de Bretagne, on the columns of the gallery; porcupines, emblems of the dukes of Orleans on the Grand Staircase ("De près comme de loin, je suis redoutable!"). An equestrian statue of the king crowns the main entrance of the château.

The gallery set against the chapel of which the southern half was destroyed during the 19th century was for many years wrongfully attributed to Charles of Orleans when it really was one of Louis XII's constructions. The greater restraint of this building is not at all surprising as it was a simple corridor connecting two main buildings and not a residential wing.

The existing chapel is the choir of the chapel built by Louis XII and dedicated in 1508 to St. Calais. The nave was destroyed during the 17th century. It was the private chapel of the royal couple. In the immediate vicinity of the castle, the vast collegiate church, St. Sauveur, was used for large ceremonies; it was destroyed after the Revolution.

The facade of the chapel, decorated with the initials of Louis XII and Queen Anne de Bretagne was redone during the 19th century. The interior is entirely in Gothic style with pointed arch vaulting, keystones and tiles with heraldic decorations.

Francis I wing. In the long series of constructions undertaken by Francis I, a prince "marvellously dedi-

cated to buildings", Blois was the first in chronological order: the Francis I wing was commenced in 1515, that is at the beginning of his reign, and works were completed before 1524, marking the death of Queen Claude de France, whose initials and emblems are associated everywhere with those of the king. Built only 15 years after the Louis XII wing, the Francis I wing is very different. During these 15 years, French art changed radically in contact with Italian art. The Francis I wing is one of the very first masterpieces of the French Renaissance.

The overall appearance of the facade looking on to the courtyard is Gothic in style on account of the lack of symmetry and due to the traditional French animation of the upper parts of the building. The steep slate roof is embellished by large chimney stacks and imposing skylights and emphasized by an openwork balustrade. But the decorative system is completly new: the windows are framed by pilasters superposed from one level to another. Their interlacing with horizontal mouldings separating the storeys gives rise to chequerwork which was very much imitated, becoming the typical order of castles of the Loire. The remarkably wide cornices bear several rows of ornaments all borrowed from Italian architecture. The Italian influence can likewise be seen in the gables of the skylights with their old-fashioned niches and their puttos. As a con-

The carved door which gives access
to Catherine de' Medici's cabinet.

Detail of the wooden panels
in Catherine de' Medici's cabinet.

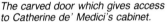 The four poster bed in Catherine de' Medici's bedroom.

cession to tradition, the emblem of the king, the sala-mander (whose motto means: "I encourage good and I stifle evil"), is sculptured eleven times in high relief on the Francis I facade.

The staircase, which was at the center of the facade before Gaston d' Orleans began to modify the château, is a masterpiece. When the Italianate straight flights of stairs appeared in the Loire Valley after the Gothic period, the shape of the spiral staircase in a protruding octagonal cage was considered rather ordinary. The originality of the solution adopted here lies in the lattice-work of the walls between the corner buttresses. This staircase, with its three floors of balconies looking on to the Court of Honor, is perfectly suitable for the display of more and more sumptuous royal ceremonies.

Gaston d'Orleans wing. The building at the back of the courtyard was built between 1635 and 1638 for Gaston d'Orleans, Louis XIII's brother, exiled to Blois due to his perpetual intrigues against the king.

The severe style of this classic building does not har-monize with the fantasy and rich decor of the Renais-sance constructions which would have disappeared if the project had been completed. The architect, Fran-

çois Mansart, had in mind a grand palace, with four wings around the courtyard and a complete rearrange-ment of the approaches with terraced gardens towards the Loire, as well as a fore-court surrounded by porti-cos, etc. This over ambitious project was abandoned in 1638. Only the wing at the back was built and even this was never completed. Gaston d'Orleans passed the rest of his life in the Francis I wing, looking out on his unfinished masterpiece.

Nowdays the Gaston d'Orleans wing houses the Municipal library and two large halls used for con-certs, conferences and exhibitions.

Francis I wing. On ascending the famous staircase to enter the Francis I wing, one notices the repetition of curved lines in the shape of the stairs, handrail, corni-ces and ribbed vault. The medallions of this vault bear the initials and emblems of Francis I, of his wife, Claude de France (the "C" and the ermine) and of his mother Louise of Savoy (the swan pierced by an arrow, the crossed wings).

The first hall one enters on the first floor is formed by two halls joined together in one during restoration in the mid-19th century. The Francis I apartments

*The assassination of the Duke of Guise
in the painting by Paul Delaroche.*

*Portrait of the three brothers of Guise
in a XVIth century painting on wood.*

King Henry III's bedroom, where the Duke of Guise was assassinated on the 23rd December 1588.

were largely restored during that period by the architect Duban: the tile flooring was redone and the walls and beams were repainted. The internal fittings were rebuilt with the exception of the chimney-pieces decorating the large hall and one of the door-frames. The elements which have been preserved are characteristic of early Renaissance sculpture: sumptuous detailed bas-relief decorations, sculptured with motifs of foliated scrolls, shells, horns of plenty and emblems.

Over a period of fifteen years, the Francis I wing was gradually renovated and furnished: Italian style tables, Flemish tapestries, chairs and, above all, chests which continued to be the basic piece of furniture during the Renaissance as in the Middle Ages.

The second hall known as the "Guardroom" features an extraordinarily large piece of embroidery dating back to the 17th century and portraying religious subjects. Two oft-reproduced portraits of the poet Ronsard, one painted and the other sculptured, can also be seen. In fact, tradition has it that it was at the castle of Blois during a ball that Ronsard met Cassandra Salviati to whom he dedicated so many poems. A wooden panel dating back to the second half of the 16th century depicts a ball at the court of the Valois which could have taken place in Blois. It mainly represents the volta, an Italian dance introduced by Catherine de' Medici.

The old building's medieval structure can clearly be seen on passing from that hall to the following gallery: door recess in the rampart 2 metres thick and rounded

sections of the tower to the right on entering. The gallery itself was also built by Francis I and opens outward mainly through sorts of loggias, variants of the loggias of Bramante at the Vatican, which in the past overlooked vast gardens.

The royal busts assembled in this gallery are a reminder of the long visits paid by Catherine de' Medici and her children to the castle of Blois during the last third of the 16th century and of the interest paid by their successor, King Henry IV, to the castle of Blois where he had a 200 meter long gallery built along the edge of the gardens; unfortunately, however, it fell to ruin during the 18th century.

At the back of the gallery one can admire a Spanish or Portuguese "Bargueño", whose numerous drawers served to stow away precious collections.

After the ante-room in an old tower dating back to the 13th century set against the rampart (note the thickness of the four walls of this room), one enters the royal bedroom occupied on several occasions by Catherine de' Medici, forced to flee from Paris which was shaken by religious troubles at the time. She died there on the 5th January 1589, a matter of days after the Duke of Guise was assassinated. This room, thus named Catherine de' Medici's bedroom, was decorated with the initials of Henry II and of the queen when it was restored during the 19th century.

During the 16th century, the room was not as private as one is made to believe nowadays. Guests were happily received there. The recess in the wall no doubt

Three rooms of the Museum of Fine Arts in Louis XII's old apartment.

enhanced the importance of the chair set on a small platform and sheltered under a dais where the queen sat. Various pieces of furniture, bought or donated over a period of fifteen years, recreate the atmosphere of a bedroom. The portraits on the walls are a reminder of Catherine de' Medici's preference for the art of portaiture whose development she encouraged during the 16th century.

The nearby chapel features interesting painted woodwork and, in the apse, one can admire an attractive piece of sculpture. The study is the most interesting room in the Francis I wing because it has kept its original carved wainscoting: its 237 panels, which are all different, offer a complete repertory of decorative motifs used at the beginning of the Renaissance: arabesques, horns of plenty, masks, dolphins, etc. This room is likewise famous on account of its secret wall-cupboards known as "poison" cupboards after the novelist Alexandre Dumas. But it is not known, in fact, whether Catherine de' Medici ever hid poison there!.

While the second floor of the Francis I wing was being renovated it was the scene of a tragic event which occupies an important place in French history. On the 23rd of December 1588, Henry, duke of Guise, was assassinated by order of King Henry III of France.

This assassination was the outcome of religious strife that ravaged France during the reigns of the children of Henry II and of Catherine de' Medici, initiated by the fanaticism of the Protestants supported by Elizabeth of England and the intransigence of the Catholics, reunited in the bosom of the League, and encouraged by Philip II of Spain. The authority of the king was perpetually combatted by this League, and in particular by its head, the Duke of Guise. The situation worsened during the meeting of the States General of the kingdom at the castle of Blois in October 1588: Henry of Guise took over and openly ridiculed the king who resolved to assassinate him. The pictures in the Cabinet room and in the king's bedroom illustrate this tragic event as well as the assassination of the Cardinal of Lorraine, brother of the Duke of Guise, which took place 24 hours later. On returning to the first floor, one reaches the hall of the States General. Let us remember that it was the great hall of the fortress of the Counts of Blois, built at the beginning of the 13th century. It was in this great hall - one of the oldest still extant in a Gothic castle -that the Count of Blois exercized his authority, dispensed justice and received the homage of his vassals. While it was part of the royal castle, it housed on two occasions, under Henry III in 1576 and 1588, the States General of the kingdom of France. The arrangement of this hall with its two naves separated by a row of columns, recalls the chapter-house of an abbey. The capitals date it back to the beginning of the 13th century. The naves are not covered by stone vaults but by a panelled ceiling consisting of small planks of wood juxtaposed. The interior decoration was repainted during the 19th century.

The elaborate facade of the castle of Brissac

▶ *View of the dining-room, with the tribune in wood that looks like marble.*

▶ *The 32 metre long Guardroom.*

BRISSAC

Once upon a time numerous windmills stood in the Brissac area, close to Angers. During the Carolingian period a local miller who used to rob wheat by making holes in his clients' sacks was given the nickname of "Brêche-sac", which was later transformed into the present day name of Brissac. Fulk Nerra, the comte d'Anjou, built a medieval castle as a military stronghold on the site and up until 1434 the various owners were all warriors. The castle was then bought by Pierre de Brézé, an important figure in the royal court who was a minister both under Charles VII and under Louis XI, and who had the building modified. The only thing that remains of this period are the two cylindrical corner towers clearly Gothic in style.

In 1502 (some say 1492) René de Cossé acquired the castle and the surrounding land. Rumor has it that Jacques de Brézé suddenly sold it as the result of the

double assassination of his wife Charlotte and her lover, of which he himself was to blame. According to certain legends, the châtelaine's ghost still haunts the castle. The religious wars had in part damaged the dwelling and it was finally transformed in 1614 by Charles II de Cossé, who held the office of marshal of France. He turned to the well-known architect Jacques Corbineau, who designed an ambitious building for his patron which, as planned, would have been unique for its times, with seven or eight floors, unusually high for buildings in the beginning of the 17th century.

Work was carried out on the central part of the old building, the towers of which were saved, until 1621. This was when death overtook Charles II, who had adhered to the Catholic League and as a faithful follower of Henry IV had opened the gates of Paris to him. The work came to a halt and the castle remained

A partial view of the Louis XIII style stone staircase.

The Mortemart room with its XVIIIth century ceiling and XVIth century four poster bed.

King Louis XIII's bedroom, where the sovereign ▶ reconciled with his mother Maria de' Medici after the battle of Ponts-de-Cé.

lower than planned and was roofed at this lower level.

The influence of Italian Renaissance art which had already made itself felt in other castles in the region of the Loire is also clearly visible here. The facades, which face the town of Brissac on one side and the park around Aubance on the other, are oriented to the east and to the north, and even though they are elegant, they lack symmetry. Tall chimneys abound on the steep slate roofs while the windows on the facades are surmounted by triangular or arched pediments, both complete and broken.

It was here that on the 12th of August, 1620, Louis XIII was reconciled with his mother Maria de' Medici, Henry IV's widow, for which the duc de Cossé organized great celebrations. The reconciliation, in the presence of representatives of the French clergy, took place in the room of Judith, after the rebel troops had been driven from Ponts-de-Cé.

In the following centuries the castle continued to belong to the Cossé family, which vaunted one of the most illustrious traditions of nobility in France. The family includes four marshals, a grand master of the artillery, five governors of Paris and many other men of state.

The apartments of the castle, lined with sculptured decoration and with richly painted beams and cross-beams on the ceilings, still contain a quantity of antique furniture and decorations. The room of Judith mentioned above contains fine polychrome tapestries and an elegant mantlepiece; the large guardroom is decorated with other tapestries as well as with military curios such as saddles and suits of armor. The dining room has a monumental staircase with two converging flights of stairs in Louis XIII style. The various rooms also contain many paintings by well known painters which portray the members of the family. The Gothic tower on the south side, part of "a new castle half built on an old castle and half destroyed" (as the duc de Cossé said regarding his residence) contains a private chapel with a marble low relief by David d'Angers, a local sculptor who worked in the first half of the 19th century.

Chateaubriand: «From a distance the building is an arabesque».

CHAMBORD

The château of Chambord is one of the loveliest Renaissance buildings in the valley of the Loire. The land on which it stands was the property of the counts of Blois, of Champagne and of Chatillon from the 10th century on, until it was bought by Louis d'Orleans in 1392. When the new duke of Orleans became king (as Louis XII) the county became the property of the crown. This elegant château was built by Francis I, Louis XII's successor, who came to the throne in 1515 when he was only 20 years old. Francis I, who was the son of Louise of Savoy, had been particularly impressed by the figure of Lorenzo the Magnificent, an outstanding personality in the field of politics and culture.

The conquest of the territory of Milan provided Francis I with the opportunity of seeing the architecture of northern Italy. As a great patron of the arts and sciences, he succeeded in bringing Leonardo da Vinci to France. The king's desire to fuse the elements of Italian Renaissance architecture with those of the French tradition in a single building was partially granted when the château of Blois was enlarged. Leonardo da Vinci worked there too in 1517 on a project for a castle that was never built. In 1519 he died in Clos-Lucé, near Amboise, it is said in the arms of Francis I who had hastened to his bedside.

It was in that year that work on the large building which was to become the king's country residence and hunting reserve was begun on the estate of Chambord on the site of an older stronghold which had been demolished to make room for the new castle. All of 1800 men worked on the château and its additions from 1526 on. The archives offer us no information as to the name of the architect but an analysis of the structures reveals a profound influence of Leonardo's thought and an extremely close tie to some of the projects by Domenico da Cortona. While in France under Charles VIII, Domenico had executed a wooden model of a castle with a square keep and large rooms in a cross plan which divided each floor into four sectors with identical apartments. One of the arms of the cross was, in the plan, taken up by straight flights of stairs which led from one floor to the next. The central keep of the château of Chambord fully respects this model and is thus related to Italian architecture and classical inspiration. The cross plan had in fact been abandoned in antiquity, and only the basilica of St. Peter's in Rome, by Bramante in 1507, had used it. The division of the floors into apartments that are separate but alike reveals the strong influence of contemporary Tuscan villas, while the large terraces and the magnificent spiral staircase in the center of the cross bear Leonardo's mark.

*Four charming pictures of the castle of Chambord,
a masterpiece in Renaissance style.*

Although this type of staircase is derived from the medieval concept, it goes far beyond it in its unique division into two separate flights with numerous openings on the arms of the corridors. A tribute to the former medieval French tradition is to be found in the presence of powerful cylindrical towers at the corners of the keep, which however harmonize with the building.

Costruction work continued for years. Around 1537 the keep was finished, in 1540 the two floors of the wing with the royal apartments were built, and the ground floor of the wing with the chapel and the walls of the annexes, while not until 1547, when Francis I died, was the wing of the royal apartments completed.

The keep, seat of the royal court, had rooms arranged in a cross plan on each of its three floors and it was here that the social life of the courtiers took place. Balls were held on the second floor, where the ceilings of the rooms were enriched with coffering and vaulting. In the sectors marked off by the arms of the cross there were four apartments per floor, in addition to another four in the corner towers. As said before, each apartment was just like the others: composed of a large hall as high as the whole floor and of two rooms, a study and a wardrobe, above which were rooms for service. Almost all the rooms (365 out of 440) had a fireplace so that each apartment could be independently heated. The double spiral staircase in the center, topped by a lantern, connected the various floors up to the top of the castle. The staircase is related to a project by Leonardo for a spiral staircase which consisted of four distinct superimposed flights of stairs, in other words just as many stairs as quarters and arms of the cross in the castle. It is therefore likely that Leonardo da Vinci's staircase, which may have been conceived for Chambord, was then simplified when it was built by the master masons of the building yard.

The top of the stairs leads to the large terraces of the castle, which again correspond to one of Leonardo's ideas, in which he intended them to be used as a place from which to admire the superstructures of the buildings. Along the walks which follow the cross plan, or those which skirt the perimeter of the wings and the towers, the members of the court could take walks and retire to observe the surrounding countryside and the hunts that were held there, as well as the decorations of the castle roof. As can be seen even from a distance, the upper part of the keep is crowded with dormer windows with Italianate classicizing superstructures, by small towers, pavilions and elegant chimneys decorated with columns, clouds, miniature pediments, salamanders and geometric motifs in slate, applied to create a two-color effect similar to that of the Italian monuments in polychrome marble. The upper part of the lantern which lies above the spiral staircase rises 32 meters up into the air. Originally open - the glass was added later - the upper part is supported by projecting

The double spiral staircase
supported by eight square pillars.

◀ The interior of the lantern over the spiral staircase and a detail of
the panelled ceiling with the salamander and the F of Francis I.

The majolica stove with the arms
of the Marshal of Saxe.

round-headed arches of medieval origin. The sculpture inside the keep, executed between 1525 and 1550, displays a profound influence of Italian classical art.

A floor plan such as that of the keep which provided for apartments that were all alike was not suitable for the royal apartments which had to be larger and more sumptuous. With this in mind the two wings for the king's rooms and for the chapel were added in 1526. Although they could obviously not have been foreseen in the original plan, the new parts seem an integral part of the keep in their style, concept and proportions. In fact these later wings used the side of the keep as the unit of measure, which was multiplied by three and by two respectively for the width and depth of the new buildings.

The royal apartments, situated in the northeast corner and in part conceived like the others, had two extra rooms. One, which was very large and long, was the official audience hall, illuminated by rows of windows like some of the rooms in the palace of Fontainebleau. The other room, more intimate and reached by means of a staircase, was a private study in Italian Renaissance style. There were two walls with windows and a coffered ceiling decorated with carvings of sala-

manders and the initial F of Francis I.

The chapel, situated to the northwest, was also profoundly influenced by Italian art and through this, by classic art: double Doric columns and pediments are combined with a large barrel vault (which in the original project had the usual coffering). The plan of the castle, in its absolute symmetry, can be symbolically interpreted: the keep, seat of the court with standardized apartments, is set between the wing of Francis I and that of the chapel, that is between the king and God. Other theories, based on the observation of the park, go even further and interpret the large trees in the woods as a symbol of the people and the circular enclosing walls of the estate, 33 kilometers long, as the symbol of the French boundaries.

The life and activity within the castle took place principally in the rooms in the arms of the cross and on the staircases. In moving from one floor to another and from one apartment to another the courtiers used the central staircase and the rooms as well as the loggias which lead to the corner towers. It was also possible to use spiral staircases in moving about between the floors, staircases which cut through the thickness of the corner towers and put the floors and the landings of

The miniature set of canons which belonged to the Duke of Bourdeaux when he was a child.

The carved wooden bed in the bedroom of the Count ▶ of Chambord made by Emile Poincon in Nantes in 1873.

the apartments in communication. They also led to the bathrooms on the ground floor. Francis I, together with his wife Eleanor, his mistress Anne de Pisseleu and the court, resided off and on in Chambord. Besides various official encounters, the king usually went there for a few weeks every two years for hunting. On the other hand, in addition to his many official obligations, he had many other hunting lodges to choose from. The considerable quantity of furnishings he brought in his wake remained in the castle only as long as the king was there. Among these were trunks, chests, bunk beds and wall hangings, including many tapestries which decorated the walls and made the rooms warmer.

In the winter of 1539, when Charles V came to stay in the castle, the baron of Montmorency (grand master of ceremonies) installed a particularly luxuriant interior decoration. The emperor, who it is said was preceded by maidens who threw flower petals in his path, admired the castle and defined it, together with the objects it contained, "a synthesis of what human industry can accomplish". Francis I, who was a connoisseur of women, included 27 young ladies of rank in his household and many more in that of the queen. Indeed he said "a court without women is like a year without spring and a spring without roses". Even so in the autumn of 1545 the melancholy king wrote the words "woman is fickle, unhappy he who trusts her" on a window pane with his diamond ring.

When Francis I died the royal residence moved to Paris. His son and successor Henry II however continued work on Chambord, realizing the second floor of the chapel and all those structures decorated with a sculptured H, his emblem. In 1552 the treaty which united the three bishoprics of Toul, Metz and Verdun, which he had previously occupied, was signed here. On his death in 1559 work on the castle stopped, although Catherine de' Medici continued to frequent the palace together with her children. Charles IX was particularly fond of hunting and many tales are told about his prowess as a hunter and a rider. It is said that he was able to follow a deer until it was exhausted without using his dogs.

After his death in 1574 the castle was practically unused for about fifty years, since Henry III and Henry IV rarely stopped there. In 1626 Louis XIII gave his brother Gaston d'Orleans the county of Blois, which included the château of Chambord. Actually this gift seems not to have been dictated so much by motives of brotherly love as by the desire to free himself of doubts as to Gaston's loyalty. The new owner immediately began to repair the residence. The tale is told of how in playing with his daughter, of whom he was particularly fond, Gaston d'Orleans agreed to climb up and down one of the flights of the large spiral staircase while his daughter ran up and down the other without

Francis I's study turned into an oratory by Queen Maria Theresa of Austria.

Interior of the chapel attributed to J. Hardouin Mansart.

ever meeting him.

Later the château once again became part of the property of the crown and Louis XIV, even though he stayed there only nine times, began important works of restoration and transformation. He abandoned Francis I's original royal wing and moved into new apartments remodelled for him in the front of the castle. New rooms on the first floor and luxurious furnishings arrived to enrich the castle from 1680 on, together with the addition of a new entrance with a pediment. The estate itself, which up to then had been covered with natural vegetation, was in part redeveloped into parks.

In 1669 Molière and Lulli wrote "Monsieur de Pourceaugnac" here and it was first presented privately for the king. It is recalled that because the leading actor was indisposed Lulli himself agreed to replace him at the last moment so as not to deprive the king of the show. Despite the fact that Lulli acted well and that there were plenty of comic situations, he noticed that Louis XIV was not laughing. Not even the lively scene of the druggists succeeded in getting the king to smile. At this points, improvising, Lulli quickly jumped off the stage, got a running start and landed with both feet on the harpsichord, smashing it to smithereens with a great racket. At this comic situation the king burst out laughing, clapping and decreeing the success of the play. The next year another work by Molière, "Le Bourgeois Gentilhomme" was presented in the castle. It is said that around

this time, here in the castle, Anne Marie Louise d'Orleans declared her love to the Duc de Lauzun by writing the name of her beloved on a mirror after having clouded the surface with her breath.

Louis XIV's new preoccupations, above all the war, put a halt to the work. It was later carried on by Stanislao Leszczynski, to whom the manor had been given by his son-in-law Louis XV in 1725. Twenty years later the castle became the property of Marshal de Saxe, the victor of Prague, Fontenoy, Rocourt and Lawfeld. The king explicitly requested that the volunteers of De Saxe's regiment be quartered in the castle. These included Poles, Hungarians, Turks and Tartars in flashy uniforms as well as the "colonel company" of negros from Martinique mounted on white Ucrainian horses. In 1750 Marshal de Saxe, mysteriously died. It is said that it was not pneumonia but rather that he fell in a duel with the prince of Conti because of the latter's wife. After his death the castle cannons were fired every quarter of an hour for six days in sign of mourning.

After having passed through other hands, the château risked being demolished after the Revolution, and in 1793 the furnishings were dispersed. The castle continued to be in a critical state under Napoleon's empire when it belonged to Marshal Berthier and successively to the duke of Bordeaux. During a visit Gustave Flaubert wrote particularly haunting lines at the sight of the empty rooms "where the spider weaves its web on the salamander of Francis I".

Despite various attempts at restoration, such as the restoration of the lantern and all the beams, the building continued in its precarious state until 1947 when the State began restorations which were to continue for thirty years and which have not yet been completed. Open to the public, the rooms of the château today contain various furnishings, including tapestries in the rooms of Louis XIV, and paintings, including the portraits of Henry III and Anne of Austria. Other rooms contain objects which belonged to the duke of Bordeaux, the comte de Chambord and last legitimate claimant to the throne of France. These include a bed and a toy battery of cannons in miniature. The ground floor contains an exhibit of the carriages built by Hermes in 1871 and which were never used. They were to have served the comte de Chambord in making his entrance into the capital to accede to the throne.

Francis I's bedroom, with the bed curtains in embroidered velvet.

Detail of a carved door and of the embroidered curtains in Francis I's bedroom.

Following pages: room where reception was held in 1681, the painting gallery and the Polish style bed in the room «of the oleanders».

The exterior of the castel of Chaumont.

CHAUMONT

The château of Chaumont (from "Chauve Mont" or Bald Hill, then changed into "Chaud Mont" or Hot Hill) stands on a hill next to the river Loire, in the midst of a dense wood of tall trees.

As far back as the Middle Ages a castle already stood here. The first owner of Chaumont was Gelduin, who was saved from having to leave the castle to his daughter Claire when a son, Geoffroi, was born to him late in life. The boy's effeminate beauty earned him the nickname of "little girl" and despite his legendary physical resistance, Geoffroi never married and was for a long time considered a hermaphrodyte. The first castle in wood was destroyed, only to be reconstructed and then destroyed once more in 1465, when Louis XI used this as a means of punishing Pierre d'Amboise - who was the owner at the time - for having sided with the League of the Common Weal. Immediately after its demolition Pierre had work begun on the present castle, which was initially meant for military use and was not nearly as comfortable as it seems now. Italian Renaissance influences which lighten the austere west wing - the oldest - are evident. The windows were added later. The other wings are more recent and reveal a more generalized Renaissance character.

Construction continued for three generations. Pierre was followed by his son Charles, the first of 17 brothers and his grandson Charles II. The reliefs at the entrance refer to Charles II who succeeded in completing the château. Two entwined C's sculptured on the circular towers which flank the drawbridge refer to him and his wife Catherine. The French coat of arms with the initials of Louis XII and his wife Anne de Bretagne is set over the entrance door while the towers bear the coats of arms of Charles II and his uncle Georges I, cardinal of Amboise. Georges was an influential figure in the court of the king where he was ambassador and prime minister. While he almost became pope after the death of Alexander VI Borgia he did in any case guarantee a brilliant career under the crown to Charles II.

In 1560, after the death of Henry II, Catherine de' Medici bought the château. A beautiful room with tapestries is in fact attributed to her. In the brief period of her occupation another Florentine was also occasionally present in Chaumont, Cosimo Ruggieri, who had come to France together with the queen. Officially an astrologer based in the Breton abbey of Saint Mahé, he may really have been a charlatan or an occultist, although some say he was a true scholar. One of his laboratories and observatories, where Ruggieri often met with the queen, can be reached through one of the towers. Some tales tell of how when the moon was full Ruggieri could see the king and his children in a magic mirror, revealing how many years they would live and how many years they would reign according to the number of revolutions the image made on the surface of the enchanted object. In any case Ruggieri was involved in various intrigues, both political and behind the scenes, prejudicial to the queen herself in whose palaces he had numerous observers. One of these conspiracies led to his detention in jail while his complices ended up on the gallows. His temporary rehabilitation

did not hinder him from returning to prison accused of witchcraft against Henry IV.

The château of Chaumont was also offered by Catherine to the lovely Diane de Poitiers, formerly Henry II's mistress, in exchange for the larger building of Chenonceaux. Actually Diane did live for a short while at Chaumont: her room - which can still be seen - and the sculptured coats of arms, identifiable by a horn, a bow and a quiver with her initials, date to this period.

Thereafter the castle passed to the Vicomte de Turenne d'Auvergne, the Duc de Saint Aignan Charles de Beauvillier, and to Jacques le Ray. Under Le Ray, during the 18th century, the Italian Nini created a factory of fine ceramics (some of the medallions are now on exhibit in the castle) in the nearby annexes. Using the clay from the Loire, Nini produced many portraits of notables which became very popular and made Le Ray a rich man. During the Empire the famous Madame de Staël whom Napoleon had enjoined to live at least 40 leagues from Paris moved to the château where she surrounded herself with sympathizers.

In the 19th century the north wing was totally demolished so as to provide a panorama of the Loire and the surrounding park. The Broglie family also had the stables with the unique conical angular construction built. In 1938 the State bought the castle. Restored and furnished, it has since then been open to the public.

◄ *Exterior and interior of the Amedée de Broglie stables at Chaumont.*

View of the castle on the Cher river.

CHENONCEAU

In 1243 the territory on which the château of Chenonceaux is built belonged to the house of Marques, originally from Auvergne. A defensive fortress surrounded by moats and joined to the banks of the river Cher with a swing bridge and a mill stood on the site of the elegant Renaissance building now to be seen.

During Charles VI's reign the owner of the fort, Jean Marques, granted asylum to an English garrison. As a result the king had the defenses dismantled but salvaged the building and left the lands to the Marquis. The family was always in debt and was forced to sell almost all its lands as time went on to Thomas Bohier, Intendent of Finance for Normandy. In the end he also bought the small fortress in 1512. However as it did not correspond to the latest Renaissance mode, Bohier decided to construct a new castle and tore down the

one that was already there. The only part that remains of the medieval part is the tower of the keep, set in front of the castle which was mostly rebuilt.

A rectangular building with angle towers, erected around an internal vestibule with ogee vaulting, was built on what remained of the mill. There were four rooms on the ground floor, while a straight staircase (the spiral staircase was generally abandoned in the early 16th century) led to the first floor where there were four more rooms. The high costs of the construction seem to explain the motto the Bohiers had sculptured together with their initials T.B.K. "S'il vient à point, me souviendra" (if the castle is finished, it will preserve my memory).

Building activity, which Catherine Bohier, Thomas's wife, had overseen in the absence of her husband, was

View of the château stretching along the river Cher, with the beautiful Catherine de' Medici gardens.

View over the gardens of Catherine de' Medici.

The castle seen from the gardens of Diane of Poitiers.

finished in 1521, when cardinal Bohier, archbishop of Bourges, consecrated the château chapel. In 1524 Thomas Bohier died in Italy in the service of the king, and only two years later his wife also died.

Inherited by their son Antoine, the castle was soon confiscated by Francis I in repayment of various deficits of which Thomas was held responsible. Some say it was expropriated in 1533 because the king wanted to come into possession of this splendid building set in the midst of an estate abounding in game. And Francis I did go to Chenonceaux, sometimes accompanied by a small group of close friends: the queen Eleanor, his son Henry, Catherine de' Medici, his mistress Anne de Pisseleu lady of Heuilly and Diane de Saint Vallier de Poitiers, his son's mistress. The castle was the scene of hunts on horseback, fêtes, suppers and intellectual activities, in accordance with the ideals of the period. Many stories, which were frequently slanderous, circu-

lated regarding Diane de Poitiers. Some said that she had conceded her favors to Henry II's father, Francis I, so that he would intercede in favor of her father; others said that Francis I had asked her to put some sense into the head of his son Henry who was still very immature, and that she had answered that she would make him her lover. Whatever the truth, Diane had great influence over Henry II and once on the throne, in 1547, even though he was married to Catherine de' Medici, he continued to shower her with gifts. Even though he was 19 years younger than Diane, the new king of France used the crescent moon (symbol of the goddess Diana) as his emblem and dressed in the colors his mistress preferred, black and white. It was not long before the château of Chenonceaux was also donated to Diane de Poitiers, despite the numerous legal cavils which decreed the building to be the property of the crown and therefore inalienable. Together

with the jewels of the crown, Henry II assigned part of the royal fiscal revenue to his mistress. With this conspicuous sum at her disposal Diane de Poitiers began the works of beautification including the layout of the garden with flowers, fruits and vegetables which at the time were considered exotic such as melons and artichokes. She also had soundings taken of the bottom of the Cher for the construction of a masonry bridge, designed by Philibert Delorme and soon built.

Despite the passing of time Diane's beauty remained unchanged, as witnessed by the painting which shows her nude next to a stag. It is said that her secret was in diving into cold water as soon as she got up, riding and walking and then going back to bed until noon. However in 1559, as Nostradamus had predicted, Henry II died after having been seriously wounded in one eye by a spear during a tournament. The queen, Catherine de' Medici, free to act as she pleased, began to vendicate herself of the lovely Diane and asked her to return the crown jewels and the castle. After attempts at resistence, Diane was forced to give in and withdrew to the château of Anet where she stayed until she died at 66 years of age. Once she had Chenonceaux, Catherine organized a great celebration in honor of her son Francis II and his wife, Mary Stuart. For these celebrations Primaticcio prepared a grandiose ornamental apparatus consisting of columns, statues, fountains, triumphal arches and obelisks, while a battery of 30 cannons was set up to fire salutes from the courtyard. New gardens, together with the annexes, were finished in 1568 and inaugurated with a great fête together with the ratification of the peace of Amboise.

Another unforgettable celebration was held in 1577 when Henry II returned from Poland for the succession to Charles IX. For the occasion the novel device invented by Henry for his festivities at Plessis-lès-Tours was used in which the women disguised themselves as men and vice versa. Henry himself wore a gown of pink and silver brocade, with violets and diamonds in his hair and pearls at his neck. The depth of his décolleté made Pierre de l'Estoile say that "it was difficult to tell at a glance if it was a king-woman or a queen-man".

Primaticcio (1504-1570) - Diane of Poitiers portrayed as a huntress.

Jean Goujon's fireplace in the bedroom of Diane of Poitiers.

XVIth century Flemish tapestry with scenes of life at the castle.

In 1580 the architect Androuet du Cerceau began work on a new wing that stretched out over the bridge on the Cher. The new building had two floors and its long facades were ably enlivened with windows, projec-tions and dormer windows. The upper floor was to be used as a ball room and was decorated like the rest of the château with rich furnishings. The sumptuous festi-vals inspired by antiquity and myths, in which the

57

ladies of the court often appeared half naked (hoping to gather useful reserved information to pass on to Catherine), ended when, in 1589, the queen mother died in Blois. Her testament entrusted the château of Chenonceaux to Louise de Vaudement, wife of her son Henry II. A few months later - in August of 1589 - Henry was killed by Jacques Clément. It is said that before he drew his last breath the king dictated a letter to his wife in which he said: "My beloved, I hope to be well: pray God for me and do not move from there". These words may have induced the queen to stay in the palace until she died. All bright furnishings were done away with and were replaced by black drapes and attributes of death. In response to her desire for prayer the Ursuline nuns came to live in the palace. She dressed in white -the color of royal mourning according to an ancient tradition - ever after until 1601 when the "White Dame" died. The château was inherited by Françoise de Mercœur, wife of Cesar, Duc de Vendôme. From then on the kings of France stopped there only rarely. The last French sovereign to stay in Chenonceaux was Louis XIV in 1650.

The state of neglect the Vendômes and the Bourbon-Condés had left the building in was briefly interrupted when one wing was used as a Capucine monastery. A drawbridge meant to isolate the monks from the rest of the world remains from this period.

In 1733 the Duc de Bourbon sold the castle to Claude Dupin, a wealthy financier. His wife, a lover of art, the sciences, letters and theater, created a bourgeois salon at Chenonceaux which included the most famous names of the time. Fontenelle, Buffon, Montesquieu, Mably, Marivaux, Voltaire, Condillac, Madame de Tency and Madame du Deffand often stayed in the castle. Jean Jacques Rousseau became Madame Dupin's secretary and tutor for her daughter. He wrote: "One passed the time well in that lovely place and one ate well: I became as fat as a friar. We made music and recited plays. I composed an opera in verse entitled "l'Allée de Sylvie" after the name of a boulevard in the park which skirts the Cher". In fact Madame Dupin had set up a small theater for the presentation of plays, as well as a laboratory for the study of physics. The rooms of the preexisting apartments had also been rebuilt and made more comfortable.

In 1782 the château came to be lived in year round by its learned owner who was so respected and loved by the local population that Chenonceaux came through the Revolution unharmed. Abbot Lecomte, local curate, intervened against the most ardent revolutionaries telling them: "There is only one bridge

left:
Catherine de' Medici's bedroom.

The Louis XIV reception room: to the left Jesus and St. John by Rubens, the Portrait of Louis XIV by Rigaud and the fireplace with the salamander and ermines, symbols of Francis 1st and of Claude of France.

right:
H. Rigaud (1659-1743) - Portrait of Louis XIV.

Carl van Loo (1705-1765) - The Three Graces.

between Montrichard and Bléré, and you want to tear it down! You are the enemies of the common good!" Madame Dupin was thus able to live in her castle until 1799 when she died at the age of 93 and was buried in the park.

Abandoned, the château was sold in 1864 by the heirs to Madame Pelouze, who started to restore the castle to what it had been before Catherine de' Medici's transformations. Although some of the windows were eliminated together with the caryatids on the facade, the monumental wing on the Cher was left untouched. The Pelouzes soon fell into ruin and in 1888 the château was confiscated by the Land Trust which sold it to Henri Menier, one of the wealthiest industrialists of the time. His brother and then his heirs are still the owners of Chenonceaux.

One of the most meritorious acts in the history of the castle was when Gaston Menier, senator of Seine-et-Marne, transformed the building in 1914 into a temporary hospital where more than two thousand wounded were recovered up to the end of World War I. After having played an important role for the crossing of the

View of the entrance hall with the characteristic triangular ribbed vaults..

The interior of the gallery overlooking the Cher by Philibert Delorme.

Bedroom of the Duke César of Vendôme, ▶
son of Henry IV and Gabrielle d'Estrées.

Bedroom of Gabrielle d'Estrées. ▶

View of the Five Queens' Bedroom.

Detail of the Five Queens Bedroom.

partisan forces in the last war, the château with its bridge over the Cher has been completely restored and can be visited.

The entrance to the estate leads through a long avenue lined with age-old trees to a vast open space on the left of which are the gardens laid out by Diane de Poitiers. In the corner of the court of honor, surrounded by the waters of the river, is the cylindrical tower which, partly rebuilt, dates back to medieval times. A drawbridge communicates with the ground floor of the castle where 16th-century tapestries are exhibited in the guardroom. Sculpture in Carrara marble, including a Virgin and Child, are to be found in the chapel. In addition to the green room and Diane de Poitiers' room, one can visit the gallery with paintings by Rubens, Primaticcio, Van Loo, Mignard and Nattier. A straight straircase leads to the first floor with the room of Gabrielle d'Estrées, the royal chamber - or of the five queens -, Catherine de' Medici's room and that of Charles de Vendôme. The original cooking area and a unique ingenious spit are still to be found in the kitchen.

*The monumental spit
in the kitchens of the castle.*

*The Waxworks Museum: King Henry II with
his favourite, Diane of Poitiers.*

In the annex, outside the château, is a small Wax Museum. The scenes reproduced include the most famous inhabitants of Chenonceaux and the most outstanding episodes in its history. Catherine Bohier is shown with a minstrel, Diane de Poitiers is in the woods during a hunt and with Henry II, Madame Dupin is shown receiving Rousseau and Voltaire, while Madame Dupin poses for the painter Nattier. There is also a reconstruction of the military hospital set up in 1914.

The elegant facade of Cheverny.

CHEVERNY

What strikes one most about Cheverny when one catches a first glimpse of it are its majesty and symmetry. It consists of a tall building joined by two wings to square pavilions covered by rounded roofs surmounted by lanterns. Its Renaissance architecture has been clearly influenced by the Classical period; this can be seen from the series of niches with busts that lighten the façade.

The castle's outbuildings house an exceptional Trophy Room, containing a collection of over two thousand deer antlers, and a kennel housing a pack sixty strong trained for coursing. The owners of Cheverny regularly organize hunts, which are greatly appreciated by hunting circles.

Unlike other castles, such as Blois and Chambord, whose interiors are almost empty, Cheverny boasts magnificent, intact furnishings dating back to the

Louis XIII epoch. In fact the castle has always benefited from the rare privelege of belonging to the same family (except for a brief period in 1564 when Diane de Potiers lived there), and this has enabled great unity of taste and style.

We know that in 1315 the castle of Cheverny was a simple press. At the time, the Hurault family was already famous; from father to son, they were secretaries, ministers and chancellors under various sovereigns, from Louis XII to Henry IV. In 1490 Jacques Hurault, Louis XII's intendant, decided to transform the press into a castle; this gave rise to a building "with a moat, drawbridge, turrets, barbicans and other forms of defence". This castle, of which only a drawing remains, appears to have been built where the outbuildings stand at present. A document relates that the existing castle built in 1634 was erected "on

The Guardroom.

The dining-room, with its walls covered in Cordova leather.

the site of the previous one", but it remains to be seen if the phrase "on the site" means "on the same site" or "in place of".

In any case, Cheverny's history is connected to a famous, dismal event, as related in the Memories of the Marquis Durfort de Cheverny, an historian, who lived in the castle during the Revolution. Henri Hurault inherited the estate in 1599 at the age of 24. At a very young age, he had married the eleven year old Françoise Chabot, but the couple had lived almost always apart because of the long military campaigns in which Henri participated. One day as a young man he was in Paris at King Henry IV's court; as a joke, he raised two fingers to look like horns above Henry's head. His gesture was met with laughter but a mirror revealed to the count that he himself was the laughing stock. Without saying a word, the young man mounted on horseback and rode until he arrived home at dawn.

In great silence, the count had the doors opened and arrived unexpectedly in his wife's bedroom; the story goes that the young page with whom the countess consoled herself over her husband's long absences, jumped out a window just in time, breaking a leg. The count killed him with his sword. Then, accompanied by a priest, he returned to his wife's bedroom, holding a glass of poison in one hand and a sword in the other, and told her that he would return within an hour, leaving the anguished woman to make the terrible decision. When the time was up, the count returned; his wife drank the poison and died. This must have been more or less how the story went, even if the parish register of St. Martin de Blois certainly gives a truer picture. In fact, it is stated that "On Saturday 26th January... the Countess de Cheverny was poisoned because she committed adultery and rumour has it that when the surgeons, William and son, opened her, they

65

The royal bedroom with its panelled
ceiling painted by Jean Mosnier.

Detail of the four poster bed in the royal ▶
bedroom, lined in XVIth century Persian silk.

discovered a five and a half month old child; the same
day a gentleman from Burgundy called Chambelin,
suspected of being her lover, was killed in the said
Castle of Cheverny". No matter what really happenend,
it remains certain that Henri Hurault, having
accomplished his terrible mission, returned to Paris the
same evening in time for the "coucher du roi"
ceremony. When the king heard about the sad events
for which in fact he was mainly responsible, he became
most irritated and exiled the count for three years to
the Cheverny estate. Here Henri Hurault fell in love

with the daughter of his Knight Commander and
married her; it was his second wife, described as being
thrifty, intelligent and with great taste, who directed
the works, enlarging and embellishing the castle; for
this purpose, she commissioned the architect Bohier
and the artist Jean Mosnier.

A direct descendant of the Huraults, the Marquis de
Vibraye then handed on the tradition to his
grandchildren, the Viscount and Viscountess de
Sigalas, who inherited the estates on his death and who
still today keep Cheverny's past splendour intact.

XVIIth century Gobelin tapestry
with the abduction of Helen of Troy.

An angle of a hall with Louis XV furniture. ▶

Detail of the large reception room, ▶
with the fireplace crowned by the Portrait
of the Countess of Cheverny by Mignard.

Detail of the Gallery, with its panels painted by Jean Mosnier. ▶

A corner of the library furnished in Early Empire style. ▶

The XVIIth century grand staircase in stone.

View of the Orangery. ▶

The Hall of Trophies, with its over 2,000 deer ▶
antlers and the stained-glass window of
Jacques Loire representing
a starting point for the hunt.

Pictures of the castle.

CHINON

This château, with its close ties to the history of France, was built for the first time in stone in 954 by Theobald I, Comte de Blois, on a steep plateau. The stronghold, which replaced a lighter wooden structure, then passed to the rival Comte d'Anjou, Geoffroi Martel, in 1044.

The comte d'Anjou was the first to join the walls of the two original defensive structures (the castles of Milieu and of Coudray) as well as adding towers and the chapel of St. Melanie. The far east wing was added by Henry II Plantagenet, who descended from the counts of Anjou and the king of England, and who called it "St. Georges's fort" dedicating it to the English patron saint. Until 1205 he and his descendants continued construction work, adding the fortress to the east and the internal chapel, the mill tower and the numerous reinforcement towers.

With the beginning of the long war with France, the English stronghold passed under the crown of Philip Augustus in June of 1205 after a months-long siege. Reconstruction was immediately begun on the towers of the Guards and of the Dogs, the new walls and the large moat which separates the western and the central blocks. Additions continued to be made up to the 15th century when the royal apartments and the great throne room were realized. The castle also included prisons where the Knights Templar, whose order had fallen in disgrace, were enclosed in 1308. The dauphin Charles made Chinon his residence. Excluded by the English, he became the "king of Bourges" and received Joan of Arc here in 1429.

The story is told of how Charles mingled with the nobles and had another person take his place. Notwithstanding, Joan recognized him in the crowd and unhesitatingly went up to him saying "Kind Dauphin, the King of Heaven asks that you be crowned at Reims and that you take Orleans...". After having assured himself that the young woman was neither mad nor possessed by the devil, Charles followed her advice and became Charles VII, defeating his adversaries.

Chinon thus became the seat of the royal government. The queen Mary of Anjou and his mistress Agnes Sorel lived here with Charles. Their apartments were connected to those of the king by an underground passage. From Chinon Charles VII reorganized France, abolishing the feudal organization, and under his reign the castle lived its moments of greatest splendor, after which it was abandoned by the court. Even so it was at Chinon that Louis XII received cardinal Cesare Borgia who had been sent by pope Alexander VI to anul the marriage of the king of France with Jeanne, who was lame and hunchbacked. Once this was done Louis XII was free to marry Anne de Bretagne, widow of Charles VIII.

The château later belonged to cardinal Richelieu, who left the stronghold to his descendants. At this point the ravages of time were augmented by man-made devastation. In 1699 the duke of Richelieu demolished Charles VII's throne room and other structures considered passé.

Neglect then led to the collapse of the roofs and pavements while various towers fell into ruin. The stones were sold as building material. After having risked total demolishment in 1854 the château has been patiently restored: the floors in the royal apartments have been recreated according to their original design and the rooms have been furnished with copies of antique furniture.

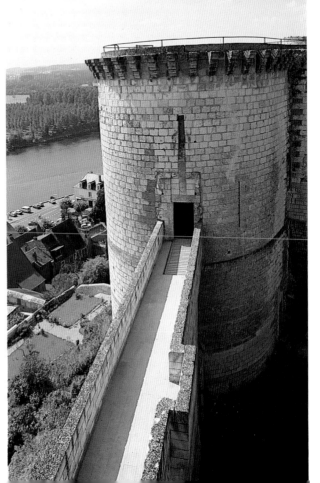

The castle seen from the lawn in front of it.

Leonardo da Vinci's kitchen. ▶

The great hall with its late XVth century ▶
furniture, where Leonardo lived.

CLOS-LUCÉ

In 1214 Sulpice III, of the house of Amboise, gave the religious community of Moncé the land on which the château of Clos-Lucé was to be built. The edifice in pink brick and white stone rose at the time of Louis XI on the foundations of a precedent construction dating to the Gallo-Roman period. It was then bought by Etienne le Loup, an enterprising scullion in the kitchens of the royal castle of Plessis-les-Tours, who in a lightning career had become one of Louis XI's favorite counselors. At the time, despite the gardens, the large dovecote in brick (still to be seen) and its vineyards, the château of Clos-Lucé was a fortified dwelling with its lookout tower, which is still in perfect condition, narrow windows, a postern and a drawbridge, traces of which are still visible next to the entrance.

When Etienne le Loup fell into disgrace, the château was bought on the 2nd of July, 1490, for 3,500 gold scudi by Charles VIII and improved, since it was now a royal residence, by skilled artisans, stone cutters and painters called in from Naples. The Chapel built in tuff for Queen Anne de Bretagne dates to this period.

A host of famous figures lived in the castle at one time or another: the young Duke d'Angoulême, the future Francis I, his sister Margaret of Navarre, who probably began to write her collection of short stories ("Heptameron") here, Louise of Savoy when she was regent, Leonardo da Vinci, as well as other notorious figures of the time including the favorite Babou de la Bourdaisiere, the captain of Henry III's guards Michel du Gast, who participated in the assassination of the duke of Guise, Saint Francis of Paola and Henry III.

The château then passed into the hands of the d'Amboise family who kept it from being destroyed in the period of the French Revolution. It has now belonged to the Saint-Bris family for several generations.

In 1955 Hubert Saint-Bris decided to restore the castle to what it looked like when Leonardo da Vinci, the most famous of its many guests, lived there.

The complex restoration was entrusted to the architect of the Monuments Historiques, Bernard Vitry, and the work to specialized craftsmen of the Beaux-Arts. Thanks to them Leonardo's kitchen, (the Old Guardroom), the Council Room and the subterranean chambers where Leonardo's splendid

The bed on which Leonardo da Vinci died.

*View of the two rooms with the models of the machines ▶
designed by Leonardo and built by I.B.M. with
period material; at the bottom,
the catapult and machine-gun.*

machines can be seen, the rooms of Margaret of Navarre and of Leonardo, each day come closer to their original appearance.

In the autumn of 1516, on the invitation of Francis I, Leonardo left Italy, accompanied by a servant and his pupil Francesco Melzi. He reached France after a long trip on muleback, bringing with him La Gioconda, St. John the Baptist and St. Anne. In exchange for the château of Clos-Lucé (which was practically next to the palace at Amboise and at the time was called Cloux) and an annuity of 700 gold scudi, the king asked nothing of Leonardo but the pleasure of his conversation. The artist however amply paid back the king by organizing memorable fêtes and fantastic spectacles, such as the one of June 17, 1518, at which Galeazzo Visconti was present and of which he left a detailed description.

The admiration and love of the court did not however distract Leonardo from his studies and drawings, which he loved more than anything else. Despite the infirmity which is said to have involved his right hand, he obstinately dedicated himself to geometry, architecture, city planning and water works.

A large number of manuscripts later than October of 1517 testify to the fervid activity of this period. These include a sheet of the Codex Atlanticus with the annotation "palazzo di Cloux d'Amboise, il 24 giugno 1518".

Probably from this period are the projects for the castle of Romorantin, those for the draining of the Sologne and those for houses which could be taken apart and which were designed specifically for the court which was always moving from one place to another.

Many drawings preserved in the Royal Library of Windsor Castle (heads of old men, sketches for fêtes and carousels and drawings of the château of Amboise seen from one of the windows of Clos-Lucé) undoubtedly date to this period.

In his will of April 23, 1519, written by the court notary, Leonardo left all his books, his drawings and the instruments relative to the art of painting to Francesco Melzi; to his servant Battista and to Salay he left, in equal parts, the land he owned in Milan; to Mathurine, the maid, a dress of black wool lined with fur, a length of wool and ducats.

He died in the château on May 2, 1519, at the age of 67, and was buried in Amboise, in the royal cloister of St-Florentin.

When the cloister was destroyed, his mortal remains were transferred to the Chapel of St-Hubert in the château of Amboise.

The exterior of Fougères-sur-Bièvre, one of the last examples of feudal architecture.

FOUGÈRES SUR BIÈVRE

Like the other châteaux of the Loire, Fougères is also situated on the area of a medieval stronghold with external defenses.

During the Hundred Years' War the castle was the scene of military action and the Black Prince destroyed a great part of it and all the defensive structures. Later, in 1470, the new owner was Pierre de Refuge, who held the office of counselor for Charles of Orleans and then, under Louis XI, treasurer to the royal court. Economically well off, Pierre was able to undertake the reconstruction of the area around the central keep which the ravages of time and man had left fairly intact. The defensive walls and the circular towers which still flank the central part were thus completed, although not by Pierre but by his successor, his son-in-law Jean de Villebresme.

As can be noted from the internal courtyard, the complex still bears signs of its medieval origin, untouched by the Italian Renaissance influences of the early 16th century. The towers are illuminated internally only by small windows - in line with the parameters of military structures - and are covered by steep conical slate roofs. The masonry construction in irregular stones and mortar differs from the more elegant structures that became fashionable later in which blocks of ashlar fit together perfectly. The low heavy arches of the courtyard lend a feeling of strength and sobriety to the entire ensemble, quite unlike the refined elegance introduced into French architecture by king Francis I when he returned from Italy. The presence of orifices for throwing molten lead, strong walls and defensive moats demonstrate that the castle was still thought of as a stronghold and not yet as a pleasant residence that was pleasing to behold and hospitable inside. Not until the 16th century were new wide windows cut into the walls of the rooms which only had enormous fireplaces. Worthy of note in the nearby town is the small church which still preserves Romanesque parts although it has been remodelled more recently.

The massive structure of the castle of Gien is reflected in the waters of the Loire.

GIEN
(International Museum of the Hunt)

The city of Gien, situated in the valley of the Loire, which is rich in game, has always been an important center for hunting and has even earned the name of "Capital of the Hunt".

Game has always been abundant in the immense forests of Orléans (34,000 hectares) which skirt the Loire from Gien to the Beauce. Gien is the northeast gate of the Sologne and the Loire is a stopping place for migratory animals.

The château of Gien was an ideal location for the creation of a Hunt Museum. The building, whose story will be briefly related, was built in 1484 on the site of a royal hunting rendez-vous by Anne de Beaujeu, eldest daughter of Louis XI and Regent of France, who had received this Crown possession from the king.

It consists of a vast building with windows that open to the south, overlooking the city at its feet, and the Loire and the countryside on the horizon. To the east another building, at right angles to the first, looks out on the river which lazily winds down towards the valley and as far as the horizon where the hills of Sancerre can just barely be distinguished.

The facades on the inner courtyard, less severe in their lines, are pleasingly embellished by three small octagonal towers in brick and stone with fine stone spiral staircases inside above which are square rooms, flanked again by round turrets which enclose narrower staircases.

When Anne de Beaujeu died, the castle returned to the Crown. Between these walls Francis I in 1523 signed the document which conferred the regency on Louise of Savoy. Henry II stayed here, as did Catherine de' Medici and Charles IX during the Religious Wars. Henry III lived here and Anne of Austria, and Louis XIV, who was then 13, sought refuge here during the battle of Bléneau in which the vicomte de Turenne came forth as victor.

The château belonged in turn to various great families until the county of Gien was suppressed during the Revolution. In 1823 the château was acquired by the department of Loiret.

The collections are lively and instructive. Chronologically arranged, they tell the story of hunting throughout the centuries by means of the hunter's weapons, as

The great hall of the Guards
in the International Hunting Museum.

Francois Desportes (1661-1743) - Studies of birds. ▶

Francois Desportes (1661-1743) - Game watchdogs. ▶

well as drawings, etchings, paintings, tapestries, decorated ceramics and accessories.

There are flintlock guns with extremely long barrels to ensure a greater firing range and to make it possible to shoot from horseback without running the risk of hitting the mount, as well as two-barrelled guns. These firearms, sculptured, engraved, damascened, inlaid with ivory, tortoise shell, mother-of-pearl or precious metals, are in themselves works of art.

The lovely room on the first floor contains more than 75 paintings and studies by François Desportes (1661-1743). Of all the rooms in the château this was the only one where this extraordinary collection could be suitably presented.

There is no doubt that Desportes was the greatest painter of animals France produced. He was assigned to the person of King Louis XIV and followed him when he went hunting, painting the finest game the king killed as well as portraits of his best dogs: Blanche, Ponne, Zette, etc. Gifted with a unique skill, he worked with an untiring virtuosity. He executed large decorations for the royal and princely houses and large hunting scenes of all kinds.

It is particularly interesting to compare the projects or studies and the large finished paintings.

Two large canvases by J. B. Oudry (1686-1755), who was Desportes' successor as painter of the king's hunts,

have been hung near the latter's paintings so that the two artists can be compared. In fact, for a long time Oudry was the better known of the two even though he seems never to have done anything comparable. An exception is his large "Wolf Hunt" in the Museum which, to experts, is one of the painter's best works.

In 1972 the Museum was presented with the exceptional collection of the personal trophies of Claude Hettier de Boislambert, Grand Chancellor of the Order of the Liberation and Honorary President of the International Hunting Council.

Claude Hettier de Boislambert was primarily interested in protecting nature and animals. He was an exemplary hunter and conceived of hunting as a rational exploitation and regulation of natural resources.

The 500 trophies on exhibition were collected in the course of 50 years of hunting as a sport. The animals to be killed were always carefully chosen and were always "approached" on foot.

An entire room is dedicated to a rare collection of 5,000 hunting buttons, small works of art created for the tunics of the supervisors of the royal hunts.

More than 50 hunting horns, set against a background of the colors of the royal hunt, trace the evolution of the horn from the time of Louis XIV to our days.

The exterior of the castle.

View of the great hall, with the monumental ▶
fireplace of Germain Pilon.

The refined furniture of the XVIIIth century ▶
in a corner of the great hall.

GUÉ-PÉAN

A few kilometers from Pontlevoy, in Loir-et-Cher, stands the château of Gué-Péan. Used as a hunting lodge, the complex dates to the 14th and 15th centuries.

The ground plan is square and it now has a gateway at the center of the encircling walls. Two low semicylindrical towers, with terraces on top, flank the entrance. Three blocks of buildings arranged in a U pattern face onto the immense court of honor. The principal block, at the back of the courtyard, is flanked by cylindrical towers with conical roofs. The rather low facade has numerous windows which mitigate the severe aspect of the castle and admit light. Elegant dormers with superstructures decorate the roof. The building block on the left, which also has dormers, is in communication with a cylindrical tower that reinforces the front corner of the walls. The tower widens near the top, with sustaining brackets, and has a helmet-

shaped dome with a small lantern, rather like the towers of the châteaux of Serrant and Valençay. The right wing, with a broad terrace, also communicates with an angle tower.

This one, quite unlike the other, is a simple cylinder with a conical roof.

Throughout the centuries numerous kings (Francis I, Henry II, Henry III) and famous men (Lafayette, Balzac) stayed in the elegant Renaissance apartments. Today the rooms of the château, which is owned by the marquis of Keguelin, are open to the public. Of particular interest are the guardroom, the chapel, the hall and the library. The rooms are furnished with fireplaces, objects of art and antique furniture in Louis XV and Louis XVI style, with tapestries and paintings (including works by A. del Sarto, J.L. David, H. Rigaud, G. Reni, J.H. Fragonard) while the library contains a valuable collection of historical documents.

The dining-room with Louis XVI period furniture.

The royal bedroom with the Louis XII period four poster bed.

Next page:

LANGEAIS

Thanks to its position on the western side of Tours, on the banks of a river, Langeais was of considerable strategic importance both as a fortress blocking access to the capital of the province as well as an outpost against aggressors from the west. Evidence of this is to be found in the ruins of Fulk Nerra's bastion which date to the 10th century and which are in what is now the park of the castle.

Only the walls on the east and north are still extant. The other two walls of the bastion, which was in the form of an elongated rectangle, were torn down in 1841.

The castle taken as a whole mirrors the soul of its builder, the fearsome Fulk Nerra, count of Anjou, nicknamed in his time "The Black Hawk". He was a typical example of the feudal outlaw: ferocious, perfidious and cynical with an insatiable lust for power. At the same time he was endowed with a superstitious piety and was famous for his excesses.

The western facade and gardens of Langeais.

His gifts as strategist and statesman permitted this founder of the Angevin dynasty to continue in power for fifty years.

When, under the reign of Hugh Capet, Fulk took possession of the holdings of Eudes I, count of Blois and of Tours, he had this fortress built as a point of support at the top of a promontory-shaped hill enclosed by the valleys of the Loire and of the Roumer at their confluence.

After his death, the house of Anjou continued its unrelenting course which was to culminate in 1154 in the consecration as King of England of Henry of Anjou, called Plantagenet. Since this great grandson of William the Conqueror had married Eleanor of Aquitaine, Langeais became one of the outposts of his immense French possessions, which included the lands of the Loire, Normandy and Aquitaine.

The Capetian monarchy at this point cuts a poor figure with regard to its vassal. In the war which followed, the Capetian monarchy was to be saved by the internal struggles of the Plantagenets which Philip Augustus skilfully manipulated. Taking advantage of the assassination of the duke of Bretagne, perpetrated by John Lackland, son of Henry Plantagenet, Philip Augustus brought him to trial before the Court of Paris and, encouraged by his victories, deprived him of his French possessions.

From this moment on Langeais was part of the royal holdings even though it was ceded various times as guarantee. This was the case in 1218 when the castle passed to Hugues X of Lusignan who had married Isabelle, widow of John Lackland.

In the course of the 13th century, custody of Langeais was entrusted successively to Guillaume des Roches, Hugues Lusignan, Alfonso of France, brother of Saint Louis, Pierre de la Brosse, Chamberlain of Philip the Bold who, accused of complicity with the king of Castile who was then at war with France, was hanged at Montfaucon in 1278.

During the Hundred Years' War, Langeais fell into the hands of the English more than once. In 1428 they abandoned it, upon receiving ransom, on condition that "the castle be torn down and razed to the ground, except the large tower".

Aware of the need of building a new fortress on this same site, Louis XI entrusted the direction of the works to his personal counselor Jean Bourré, who also held the office of "Captain of Langeais".

Jean Briçonnet, General of Finances, mayor of Tours, was set in charge of payments for the works and construction of the castle of Langeais in 1465 and 1467. With its high walls and its narrow cross-bar windows, its three round towers and its encircling wall of machicolations and crenellations, the new building is the perfect picture of an imposing austere fortress. One of the characteristics of this facade is the continuity of the sentinel walk which surrounds the entire building, towers included, for a length of 130

View from above of the interior of the chapel.

*The Guardroom with its two bronze
light fittings by A. Dürer.*

meters, always on the same level. The king's purpose in rebuilding this castle was that of protecting to the west the royal residences of Tours, Plessis-les-Tours and Amboise, which were vital to his government. To the east they were protected by Chaumont and to the south by Chinon and Loches.

On the 16th of December, 1491, the castle of Langeais was the stage for an event that was to make it more famous than any other castle - the wedding of Charles VIII and Anne de Bretagne, as a result of which Brittany was annexed to France. This union was to throw European politics into confusion. The duchess Anne had already been married by proxy to Maximilian of Austria, Emperor of the Holy Roman Empire, and Charles VIII was engaged to his daughter, Margaret of Austria, who with this wedding in mind had been brought up at the court of France. The union had been planned by the regent Anne de Beaujeu who wanted to unite Brittany to the French kingdom and was conscious of the danger of letting it fall into the hands of the Emperor (even if, as duke of Bretagne, he was a vassal of the king). "Since Charles was of the opinion", says Brantôme, "that it was not a good idea to have such a powerful lord in his own realm, he took Anne from Maximilian, her promised spouse, and married her".

The situation had precipitated. Charles VIII did not

present himself to the duchess at Rennes, which was besieged by French troops, until a few days before. In order to escape the opposing party, the princess arrived secretly at the castle of Langeais, where the king was waiting for her. This wedding was more like a kidnapping than anything else.

The most important clauses in the wedding contract were the unification of Brittany with France, and, to ensure this union, the obligation on the part of the queen, if the king died before she did and left no heirs, to marry his successor. And this was just what happened. A second marriage made her the wife of Louis XII. The chroniclers of the time have left us fantastic accounts of the pomp and magnificence of the wedding.

After this, Langeais disappears from History with a capital H. As an aside, let it be remembered that Charles IX stayed at the castle on November 19, 1565, and Louis XIII in the early days of October 1627, on the journey which took him to the siege of La Rochelle.

In 1631 the castle, which up to this time had been ceded to various persons only as a pledge - the holder had only the use while the property legally remained in the king's possession - was given to Louise of Lorraine, daughter of the duke of Guise, who ceded it almost immediately to the marshal Marquis d'Effiat, baron of Cinq-Mars and father of Louis XIII's favorite, who was beheaded in 1642. In 1765 the descendants of Marquis d'Effiat ceded it to the baron of Champchevrier, but it went instead to the duke of Luynes who exercised his preferential right.

The château came through the Revolution intact, and in 1797 it was acquired by a bourgeois of Tours, Charles-François Moisant, who left it in a state of abandon.

Houses were built right against the walls of the castle and the finest hall on the ground floor was transformed into a stable for the gendarmes.

Bought in 1839 by a Parisian lawyer, Christophe Baron, the building underwent radical restoration. Some of this was the work of fantasy, such as the extension of the machicolations to the entire facade of the internal courtyard, or the crenellations which decorated the ridges of the roof.

Jacques Siegfried, who bought it in 1886, set about to restructure it fundamentally. The most important aspect was the restoration of the interior of the château, to which he dedicated twenty years of his life.

The unity of style, which the castle owed to the speed with which it had been built, survived the centuries.

The carved wooden door which provides access to the marriage room.

The hall where the wedding of Charles VIII and Anne de Bretagne was held in 1491.

XVth century
tapestry from
Bruges with
the Crucifixion.

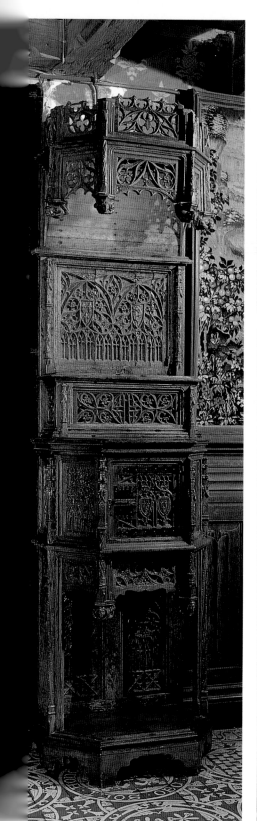

Sideboard crowned by a canopy with
the inlaid coats-of-arms of
Charles VIII and Anne of Brittany.

Tablet attributed to Duccio
with the Madonna and Child.

Bedroom of the Monsieur with the famous tapestry «aux aristoloches».

Since the people who had lived there up to 1641 had not been the owners, but had only enjoyed the use of the building, they had not been interested in shouldering the costs of bringing up to date a building which remained the king's property. In the following periods the dimensions and the solidity of the construction probably discouraged any unwarranted desire for changes. While this may have been true of the exterior it was not the case with the inside and Jacques Siegfried, who worshipped the past and took the castle to heart, set out to restore the interior of the monument to what it must have looked like when it was built.

With this end in mind he engaged a talented young architect, Lucien Roy, and the most famous archaeologists such as Palustre, Foulc, Spitzer, Peyre and Bonnafé. Their attempts to be as historically exact as possible led them to search particularly for elements of flamboyant Gothic style. The furniture and wood panelling is either authentic or copied from originals. The pavements, which differ from room to room, were designed on examples of the 15th century or copied from period paintings. They are the most noteworthy aspect of the restructuration, for the furniture, with few exceptions, is all period furniture. Wardrobes, chests, bureaus are either 15th- century or Renaissance.

But the highlight of the interior decoration is the marvelous collection of 14th- and 15th-century tapestries - over thirty - which Jacques Siegfried put together between 1888 and 1900.

The oldest pieces, including various millefleur and a splendid Crucifixion, are Flemish while the others are mostly Aubusson. The greater part date to the 16th century but are still in Gothic style, like the hunt scenes, the story of Nabucodonosor, the curious "Miracles due to the intervention of the Holy Sacrament".

The intrinsic value of these works of art, including sculpture and paintings, is intensified by the fact that they harmonize perfectly with the furniture. This inviting and lived-in aspect of the château strikes the visitor in sharp contrast to the forbidding aspect of the fortress from outside.

*Detail of the early XVIth century Flemish
tapesty called «aux aristoloches».*

In 1904 Jacques Siegfried offered to donate the château and his collections to the French Institute. For fear that this example of the national patrimony might be bought by some wealthy art lover from the New World and transported stone by stone to America, the Institute decided to accept the financial burden that maintaining a monument of similar size entailed.

Actually the continuous growth of tourism and the position of Langeais on the route of the châteaux of the Loire were to provide the Siegfried Foundation with the means not only to maintain the monument but also to provide for the periodic restoration required. The French Institute sees to it that its management is completely autonomous, with the aid -for some of the works of restoration - of the Caisse Nationale des Monuments Historiques et des Sites.

In 1924, and again in 1938, Jacques Siegfried's daughter, Agnes, completed her father's work, donating the large park which, beyond the ruins of Fulk Nerra's tower, dominates the valley of the Loire to the west - with the houses which climb up the slopes of the hill - and on the northwest the road that leads to the upland plain.

The monument is thus amply protected on this side. To the east and to the north, the old city embraces the château and provides a suitable environment.

In line with the spirit of the donor and its own principles the French Institute promises to perservere and continue his work.

Next page:

LE LUDE

The first castle to be built here, known at the time as Castellum Lusdi, was in wood as was customary in the Middle Ages. It was part of the property of the counts of Anjou and was rebuilt in stone in the times of Fulk Nerra. A legend narrates that this was when the Loire was canalized and its course was deviated several kilometers to bring it closer to the castle while the old river bed became a brook. Another legend of the same period refers to the fact that in the 10th century a demon inhabited the castle. In the guise of a servant he attempted to kill the owner. It was necessary to call in a bishop, Breviliguet, who used exorcisms to get rid of Satan's emissary. Remembrance of this event is to be found in the name of the westernmost tower of the castle, which has been known since then as the "Devil's tower".

Remodelling in the 13th century gave the fort a keep with walls, six towers and a deep moat. All that is left today of these structures is a subterranean vaulted room.

This defensive outpost on the Loire was acquired by the Vendôme family in 1378 but they abandoned it in

Two views of the castle.

the face of the relentless pursuit of the English troops under the count of Warwick. In 1427 the stronghold was reconquered by Amboise de Loré and Gilles de Rais. Despite the fact that he was a Marshal of France, the latter was unable to escape the gallows after having been condemned for satanic rites during which he supposedly had hundreds of children killed.

The new owner from 1477 on, Jean II Daillon, sided with the faction that opposed the French dauphin. After Louis XI became king he pursued Jean for a long time and forced him to hide for seven years in a cave. Reconciled with the king, Daillon obtained important offices in court and was able to turn his attentions to the transformation of the castle into a building with three arms around a central court of honor. The work of restructuration was completed by Jean II's two successors, both of whom were valorous soldiers. Louis XII's wing, Francis I's wing - with architectural ornaments of Renaissance nature - and the gardens laid out on the area of the old moat were thus added on to Le Lude. Other transformations took place in the following centuries, such as the addition of a monumental facade towards the Loire, in Louis XVI style, and the large triangular pediment on the new building block. Inside there was space for numerous reception halls and private rooms, while various antique furnishings and a large library are now in the other wings.

The facade of the royal apartments.

LOCHES

The history of the château of Loches is intimately tied to the history of France as far back as the 10th century. At that time a wooden tower for defense rose on the highest point of a rocky plateau. It was connected to the surrounding countryside by tunnels excavated in the rock. At the beginning of that century the feudal domain belonged to Fulk I the Red, comte d'Anjou, whose descendant Fulk Nerra created one of the first square forts in stone here.

Fulk Nerra made a name for himself in French history as a warrior. He was already count at the age of 17 and spent all his life feuding with the neighboring counts of Blois. Despite the fact that he was the son of Fulk the Good (a man of learning and of wit, famous for his phrase to Louis V "an ignorant king is nothing but an ass with a crown"), Nerra sullied himself with more than one sin and went on pilgrimage to Jerusalem three times to expiate.

Aside from this, the birth of military architecture in stone owes a great deal to Fulk Nerra. He was a great builder of defensive works and realized several dozen forts based on the new dictates which at the time made them impregnable. The tower at Loches, with a base measuring 25 by 15 meters, was built between 1005 and 1070. Over 38 meters high, its walls, between two and three meters thick, are still pierced by holes for the

scaffolding that was erected when it was built as well as holes for the suspension of the battlement platforms, wooden structures which were suspended in the void and from which projectiles were hurled at the attackers. The three floors inside had chimneys whose vents can be seen from the outside.

In 1040 Nerra died at Loches where he was buried and his successor Geoffroi Martel of Anjou succeeded in defeating the counts of Blois at S. Martin-le-Beau.

The house of Anjou thus came into possession of Loches - where other defenses were built towards the south - and the surrounding territory at their disposal, until the last of the Fulks married the daughter of the duke of Normandy, king of England. Their son, Henry Plantagenet, also became king of England in 1154. But it was not long before disagreements arose between him and Philip Augustus, king of France, who took a large part of their dominions from the Plantagenets. When Henry II Plantagenet died, his son Richard the Lion-Hearted went to the Holy Land for the Third Crusade. Upon his return he fell prisoner to the emperor Henry VI of Austria and Philip Augustus was able to obtain various territories including Loches from Richard's brother, John Lackland. Free once more, Richard the Lion-Hearted recaptured Loches in 1195 after only three hours of fighting. He died barely

Two views of the entrance to the royal apartments.

four years later in Chinon. His legitimate heir, Arthur, was assassinated by John Lackland against whom Philip Augustus of France moved once more, taking Loches in 1205 after a year-long siege.

The crown of France, which has owned the castle since then, incremented the defenses adding the Vieux Logis to the north, with a tower and a sentinel's walk, in the 13th century. In June 1429, after the taking of Orleans, Joan of Arc arrived here to convince Charles VII to move on Reims and be crowned king. And it was this same Charles VII who in 1444 had Agnes Sorel, the lovely lady-in-waiting who became the first mistress of a king in the history of France, stay in one of the towers here. Known as the lady of Beauté (both for her beauty as well as for the estate of Beauté-en-Champagne given to her by the king), Agnes was only twenty when Charles, in his forties, fell in love with her. Agnes took an interest in the affairs of court and loved to surround herself with luxury, so that the king often gave her jewels and rare oriental products. Despite this she was very devout and was a benefactress of the local church of Notre-Dame in Loches, today known as Saint-Ours.

This church had been built on the land belonging to the fort between the 11th and 12th centuries. Palmettes, human figures, monsters and animals of

DANS CETTE SALLE
LES 3-5 JUIN 1429
JEANNE D'ARC
VINT PRESSER
CHARLES VII
DE SE FAIRE SACRER
POUR ÊTRE SAUER
ROI DE FRANCE

AGNÈS SOREL

obvious Romanesque origin decorate the portal above which is an Adoration of the Magi. At present the interior dates in part to the 11th century and in part to the 14th and 15th centuries.

Agnes died in 1450, only 28 years old, apparently due to complications arising from a difficult pregnancy. Even so rumors were that she had been poisoned by the dauphin who had tried to seduce her, forcing her to leave Chinon for Loches. Agnes requested that she be buried in the church she had endowed and to which she left an inheritance of 2000 gold scudi. With the accession of Louis IX the monks asked to be allowed to transfer the mortal remains of the king's mistress from the church to the castle since a sinner could not be buried in a holy place, but the threat of having to return the gifts she had bestowed made the monks think twice and the tomb of the lady of Beauté, with its sculpture and its alabaster, remained in the church up to the French revolution.

◀ The «conversation» room, where Joan of Ark met the Dauphin Charles.

◀ Alexandre Millin du Perreux (1764-1843) - Joan of Ark meeting Charles VII at Loches.

◀ Copy of Francois Clouet - Portrait of Agnès Sorel.

XVth century armour.

◀ *The tomb of Agnès Sorel, Charles VII's favourite, taken full lenght and in detail.*

Stained-glass window with the coat-of-arms and initial of Agnès Sorel, Charles VII's favourite.

During the 15th century the kings of France completed the Vieux Logis with new dwelling constructions, with the New Tower and the Martelet. The Logis Royaux thus was eventually comprised of a tower and a wall of the 13th century, a block of constructions with a guard tower of the 14th century, and a hunting pavilion of the 15th century, contemporary with still another bastion in which passageways for various streets were opened (Porte des Cordeliers, tower of St. Anthony).

The new wing contains the chapel of Anne de Bretagne, wife first of Charles VIII and then of Louis XII. When she was only 23, Anne had already suffered the loss of her parents, her husband and four children. The queen was fond of retiring into a small room she had had prepared in Loches where she could pray. Silver Breton ermelines were sculptured on the walls on a blue ground, and an altar and a fireplace decorated the corners of the room.

History narrates that during the Revolution the insurgents penetrated the château of Loches and devastated the Logis Royaux and Anne's chapel, as well as the prisons and the church of Notre Dame. Here, mistaking the rich tomb of Agnes Sorel for that of a saint, they vented their wrath and destroyed it. Later the

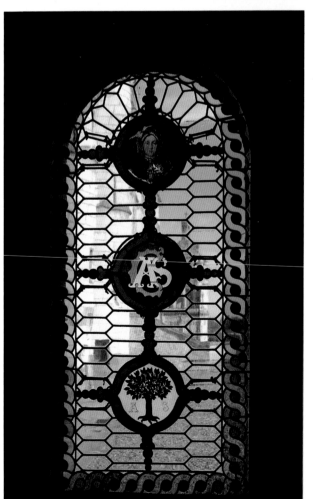

School of Jean Fouquet: Triptych of the Crucifixion dated 1485 from the Carthusian Monastery in Liget.

The private chapel of Anne of Brittany, decorated with silver ermines (the symbol of Brittany) and with the cord of St. Francis.

remains of Agnes were transferred to the castle and her tomb is now in one of the rooms of the Logis Royaux. The sculptured tombstone there is a copy of the alabaster original. It shows the lady of Beauté with her hands joined, watched over by two small angels and with two lambs at her feet.

Part of the castle of Loches was used as a prison and many famous personages occupied the cells from the 15th century on. In 1469 Cardinal de la Balue was imprisoned in the circular tower. He had conspired against king Louis XI, causing him to be taken prisoner by Charles the Bold. Still today it is remembered that the cardinal was enclosed in a cage which he himself, the height of irony, had invented and which was known as the "little girl" because it was so small (1.50x1.75 m). Suspended beams and pulleys permitted the cage to be suspended several meters above the ground at night to avoid the possibility of flight.

Philippe de Commynes, famous historian, was also imprisoned in Loches. He betrayed Louis XI, embracing the cause of the nobles who had opposed the king. Transferred to the prison in Paris, he was finally rehabilitated under Charles VIII. Ludovico Sforza known as il Moro, duke of Milan, was also detained in the

Two views of the imposing tower.

Martelet. This refined scholar had been taken prisoner at the battle of Novara and after an initial period in Bourges he was confined to Loches. Because of his rank Louis XII permitted him to have various comforts such as the company of a court jester and of teachers and the use of furniture and a fireplace. He himself decorated the walls and barrel vault of the cell with a helmet, snakes, stars and various mottos (including "He who is not content"). For eight years, up to 1508, il Moro remained closed in this room. It is said that as soon as he was freed, he died at the sight of the light and open air.

Other rooms were occupied by Antoine de Chabannes and Jacques Hurault, bishops of Le Puy and of Autun, who took part in the plot against Francis I related to the revolt of the high constable Bourbon. The two prelates carved an altar and a via Crucis on the walls of their cell during their stay in prison.

Many old tales tell of the innumerable rooms and subterranean caves (from which the rock had originally been quarried) under the castle of Loches. One of these tells of a governor of Loches, Pontbrilliant, who attempted to visit all the rooms of the castle and forced some of the ancient doors which he found barred. Following various underground galleries which went deeper and deeper into the rock, the governor reached a last door beyond which he found a room where he saw a tall man seated with his head between his hands.

The Romanesque church of St. Ours.

The sumptuous decoration of the Romanesque portal of the Church of St. Ours.

◀ The torture room.

◀ The frescoed prison of Ludovico Sforza called the Moor.

When he came closer, he realized that it was a cadaver which the air of the closed room had mummified. The wind from outside reduced the body and a coffer which contained carefully folded garments into dust. Some say this tale is not a legend at all but really happened for some of the bones of the cadaver were exhibited in the church of Notre-Dame.

One of the rooms in the dungeons of the castle that can be visited is the so-called interrogation room, the ancient torture room. Created in the middle of the 15th century by Charles VII, it still preserves the bar with rings which imprisoned the ankles of the prisoners when they were slowly torn to pieces until they confessed their crimes. Ironizing on the harshness of the treatment an inscription in the circular tower says "Enter, gentlemen, to the king, our Lord".

A charming picture of the castle.

The collection of trophies in the hunting room. ▶

A view of the saddlery which houses ▶
old coaches and one-horse carriages.

MONTPOUPON

This château rises in an isolated position between the valleys of the Indre and of the Cher. It stands in a clearing at the conjunction of three small valleys which are traversed by five brooks. The road that connects Loches with Montrichard passes by the front of the building which has a particularly elegant aspect.

The castle was begun in the 12th-13th centuries, as indicated by the oldest extant parts. The cylindrical keep which widens slightly at the base dates to this period. This massive structure is typically medieval in the limited number of narrow windows which appear only above a determined height, in the widening of the summit and the stone bracket supports, and in the presence of small windows and arrowslits on top.

A long wing for the apartments is set against the keep with its conical roof. The diversity of architectural concept identifies them as 15th- and 16th-century additions. True symmetry is lacking in the facade of the château which is marked by a play of dark and light in which the masonry of the walls contrasts with the lighter color of the corner stones and of the reinforcements at the windows. The left side terminates in a slender angle tower, with elongated windows with architraves, thus balancing the tower of the keep which rises behind it. The right side consists of a wing with lodgings characterized by faceted polygonal stonework. Dormers with triangular decorative superstructures are set into the high pitched slate roofs of the central block. The whole complex is surrounded by a low encircling wall which incorporates a cylindrical tower with a conical roof and a postern dating to the 16th century. Square in form, the latter has angle towers (the ones on the facade are set on jutting corbels) between which is the portal, a window, and a dormer. The gate leads to the court of honor with the castle well.

The building was originally used by gentlemen when they went hunting and for a long time it belonged to the de Prie family, which included Louise de Prie, governess of the French heirs to the throne. Today the manor belongs to the family of de la Motte Saint-Pierre.

Two views of the châtelet, the oldest part of Montreuil-Bellay.

MONTREUIL-BELLAY

Like many other castles of the Loire, Montreuil was also built on the orders of the count of Anjou, Fulk Nerra. This 11th-century warrior was a tireless builder and he had the castle set on a steep slope where it would be easier to defend.

The manor was given by Fulk to a vassal, Berlay (or Du Bellay), who gave his name to the location. Montreuil seems to be derived from the Latin Monasteriolum, with reference to the small monastery the Du Bellays had built near the stronghold. Du Bellay I was followed by a long line of descendants: the tale is told of how during a hunting expedition near Brossay,

Du Bellay I was charged by a large boar. Without weapons, which he had left lying on the ground, Du Bellay was about to fall under the tusks of the animal when he invoked "Saint Hubert! Saint Hubert!" and succeeded in putting the animal to flight. Because of the prodigious event the Du Bellay family from then on used the motto "Hubert! Hubert!" as its battle cry.

At that time the castle consisted of a tall main tower surrounded by moats, and a double circle of walls protected by barbicans. This layout turned out to be essential in resisting sieges around 1150 when the Plantagenet king of England moved against the Du Bellays. All

105

A corner of the castle kitchens.

of them, particularly Giraut Du Bellay, had opposed the counts of Anjou, who repaid them sacking the valley of the Thouet and laying siege to the castle.

After a few months, despite the destruction of the walls, the siege slackened and the situation ended in a stalemate. The besieged had sought refuge in the main tower, impregnable thanks to the moats, and here, blessed with the use of a mill, a well and an oven, they were able to resist for a long time. Morover, subterranean passages permitted the Du Bellays to communicate with the fort of La Motte-Bourbon, while another underground passage, leading north, may have passed under the Thouet and surfaced near the abbey of Asnières. In the end the comte d'Anjou won out and the keep was semi-destroyed. The victory was accompanied by a sinister prediction made by the prior of Brossay, who warned him of his imminent death. And indeed, shortly thereafter, he took a bath in the waters near Château-du-Loir, because of the great heat, and came down with a fever which killed him in a few days, during which he refused confession even as he was dying. Giraut Du Bellay, who survived the fall of the castle, also died soon thereafter and in 1155 was buried in the church near the abbey of Asnières which he had built. Despite the fact that this building was devastated by the Huguenots, a magnificent 13th-century choir still exists.

One of the most illustrious descendants of the Du Bellay family was Guillaume Du Bellay, a warrior and governor of Turin and Piedmont who used a network of informers spread throughout the courts of Europe in explicating his diplomatic activity. His brother Jean was also active in this field. As a cardinal he lived at length in Rome with his nephew Joachim. The latter, a subtle poet, left us his sense of nostalgia for his country and for the buildings in the Loire valley in some of his verses: "I like best the dwellings built by my ancestors... I like sharp slate more than hard marble".

The new lords of Montreuil, the Melun-Tancarville and the d'Harcourt, built the defenses of the city in the 15th century with a circle of walls and gates of which only four are still to be seen: Porte du Moulin, Porte Saint-Jean, Porte de Boële and Porte Neuve.

Thanks to the testament and the money of the d'Harcourts the castle of Montereuil-Bellamy received its present aspect.

View of the dining-room.

The music-room, with its XVIIIth century furniture.

The flamboyant Gothic style chapel houses interesting XVth century frescoes.

The entrance consists of the Châtelet, in the area of the older buildings, followed by the Petit-Château (with four apartments meant for the canons of the chapter) and the Château-Neuf. A square building with low ogee arches, situated in an internal court between the Petit-Château and the Château-Neuf contains the enormous kitchen. A walkway connects this room to the Château-Neuf, with its fine internal staircase which the duchess of Longueville mounted on horseback. Besides the chapel, with its fine frescoes, the base of a pyramid is to be found in the castle - at the base of the western towers of the fort - whose purpose is still a mystery.

The exterior of Montsoreau.

The room of the military relics of the Moroccan Goums. ▶

The Guardroom. ▶

MONTSOREAU

Today the château of Montsoreau stands a few meters from the banks of the Loire. When it was built, in the 15th century, the waters of the river lapped its front. In 1820 the embankments were widened. For Jean de Chambes, the builder and an important personage in the court of Charles VII, it served as a point from which to control the various routes which crossed the area, including that of the pilgrims on their way to the abbey of Fontevrault.

The most famous figure in the history of the castle is without doubt Charles de Chambes immortalized in "La Dame de Monsoreau" by Alexandre Dumas père. Written three centuries after the facts to which it refers took place, the tale was based on the story of Charles, his wife Françoise (and not Diane) and the latter's lover, the lord of Bussy. Françoise de Meridor had taken as her second husband Charles, the duke of Alençon's chief hunter, who, in spite of the tale, was not old, but about the same age as his wife and quite handsome. In the castle of Coutancière, Françoise de Meridor met Louis de Clermont d'Amboise, lord of Bussy and favorite of the duke of Alençon. He is remembered as being "handsome, with a fine face, clear eyes, a commanding, often seductive, glance" and as a courageous and cultured warrior, a reader of Plutarch. His figure and his often unscrupulous attitudes made him various enemies and in 1579 the lord of Bussy decided to retire to his estate and left the court. This was when he courted the lady of Montsoreau. He boasted of his success - whether or not it corresponded to the truth - in a letter to a friend at court, to whom he wrote "I have caught the master hunter's deer in my nets". The rumor soon reached the ears of De Chambes who hurried to the castle and forced his wife, who professed her innocence, to write a note to her presumed lover inviting him to a tryst in the castle of Coutancière. The mortal trap had been sprung. Louis de Bussy showed up at the appointment with only one friend and as soon as he entered the castle the doors were blocked to prevent his escape. Attacked by a dozen men he defended himself to his last breath and, about to throw himself out the window, he was killed. The ending of the tale is much more prosaic than expected, for his death was received with indifference by Françoise de Meridor who, reconciled with her husband, presented him with several children.

Today the castle also houses a museum with the military curios of the Goums, a corps of Morocco troops founded by General d'Amade, which fought in the Italian campaign of World War II as well as in Morocco.

A picture of the castle on the left bank of the Loire.

Horse museum: a magnificent example ▶
of a XVIIIth century Russian
sleigh in wood and leather.

SAUMUR

Once upon a time there was a lovely castle, a vacation residence, so beautiful that René of Anjou, the poet king, chose this above all others as the Castle of Love in his romance *Le Coeur d'Amour Epris...*

"The four walls of this lovely castle were of crystal and at the top of each corner there was a large tower made of ruby stones, fine and resplendent, the smallest of which was larger than the body of a man. And these towers were covered with platinum, as thick as the palm of a hand, and the constructions between these towers were covered with fine gold tiles, exquisitely enameled with the motto of the God of Love - "A coeur volage"... And to make things even clearer, this lovely castle looked just like château of Saumur in Anjou which lies along the river Loire".

Thereafter various buildings arose on the emerald rock: one built by Thibault le Tricheur, comte de Bois, and later taken over by the terrible comte d'Anjou, Fulk Nerra, and one built by Goeffrey Plantagenet of which remains may still exist at the base of the southeast wing. But the story of the present castle begins with the one built by Saint Louis.

Saumur belonged first to the counts of Blois, then to the house of Anjou and then to the king of France. In 1203 Philip Augustus, rival of the Plantagenets, took over the castle and incorporated it and the territory it controlled into the royal possessions.

Historians place the construction of a fortress at Saumur between 1227 and 1230 when Blanche of Castile was queen regent. The fortress was to serve the Crown in reconquering Angers and that part of Anjou which it had just lost with the Treaty of Vendôme.

Its usefulness from a military point of view lasted only two years, for Angers once more became the royal seat and Saint Louis constructed an enormous fortress there which is still extant.

His castle at Saumur was in the shape of an irregular square with a round tower at each corner and it was approximately oriented towards the four cardinal points. The south tower and the west tower still retain almost all of their foundations dating to the 13th century and the original six-ribbed vaulting on the ground floor. The east tower was restructured externally but its vaults are more elaborate and the keystone is decorated with the Anjou coat of arms.

Not until the second half of the 14th century was the elementary building of the time of Saint Louis transformed into a vacation residence, under Louis I of Anjou, second son of King John I, who received Anjou in appanage in 1360 and which was then transformed into a duchy.

Louis I did not destroy the fortress his ancestor had built but he did transform it. He used the same ground plan with the round towers as foundations for

Horse museum: The Saumur cavalry school
in an etching by Victor Adam.

Museum of Decorative Arts - early XVIIIth century ▶
Brussels tapestry after Jordaens cartoons
and portraying Monsieur de Pluvinel
and Louis XIII in his youth.

polygonal towers with high buttresses which supported the sentinel walks of the crenellated machicolations.

The entrance tower as it looks now with its projecting guardhouses appears in the miniature of the month of September in the *Très riches heures du Duc de Berry*.

We know that "good king René", grandson of Louis I of Anjou, had sung the praises of Saumur as a Castle of Love and had left his mark on it.

The accounts and diaries of his director of works, which are preserved in the National Archives, reveal that the construction work on the castle must have been important to judge from the time involved (from 1454 to 1472) and the cost. Still extant parts dating to the time of King René include two small vaulted rooms in the square tower next to the large tower, the oratory on the first floor with the coats of arms carved on the keystone, and "the corridor which leads from the staircase to the tower" with love-knots carved on the keystone which must have been done in honor of Jeanne de Laval who married in 1454.

At the death of King René, in 1480, the duchy of Anjou returned to the Crown and the castle of Saumur came to house a royal garrison. A century later the Reformation modified the destiny of the castle: King Henry III was forced to ask the king of Navarre for help in saving his throne and concluded a truce with him. With the Treaty of Tours, he ceded Saumur, where there were many Protestants. The future Henry IV named his ambassador and friend, Philippe Duplessis-Mornay, who was in charge of the negotiations, as military governor general.

On April 15, 1589, Duplessis-Mornay entered Saumur and installed his garrison. The next day the king of Navarre in turn entered the city, extremely satisfied to have taken over this key site on the Loire. He ordered the new governor to fortify the fortress "with all diligence and without trying to economize" and left him Bartholomeo, his engineer, to plan and follow the works.

In addition to the fortifications around the city, he had the projecting walls and bastions, which still surround the castle and are faced in cut stone, built. Unfortunately this wall has lost most of its projecting look-out towers which kept the protruding corners of the bastions under surveillance.

When he arrived in Saumur, Duplessis-Mornay and his family went to live in a "town house" at number 45 Grande Rue, which at the time was quite new and comfortable, for the "castle was all in ruins". However in 1596, after "some of the inhabitants of the town had attempted to kidnap him and make him leave the place", he decided to move to the stronghold which he first had to repair at great cost to make it habitable.

A man of war and a shrewd diplomat, Duplessis-Mornay was also a learned theologian. In 1593 he founded a Protestant Academy in Saumur which was to bring fame to the city for almost a hundred years. Governor of Saumur for 32 years, he was a faithful servant of the Crown under two kings. Despite this, in 1621 he fell into disgrace when Louis XIII replaced him with a Catholic governor.

The political and military role of the castle thus came to an end. From then on, it began a less glorious

epoch. For almost two centuries the old fortress, whose buildings were abandoned and gradually fell into ruin, was used as a gilded prison for various hare-brained individuals or gentlemen of rank who had been imprisoned by the king. Their treatment was anything but harsh. Accompanied by a valet or a more important following they were often allowed to go out into the city. The King's lieutenant who commanded the fort frequently invited them to his table.

In 1768 the Marquis de Sade lived at the castle for a fortnight before being imprisoned at Pierre-Encise (near Lyon). Admiral de Kerguélen-Trémarec, explorer of the Indian Ocean, served four years imprisonment here (1774-1778), condemned for having abandoned a ship at sea, after he had returned from an unlucky expedition.

In 1779, during the American War of Independence, 800 English prisoners were enclosed in the manor as well as in the chapel of the building on the square and in other "annexes" on the bastions. Most of these were sailors as can be gathered from the graffiti they left where their names and the date of their capture are often accompanied by the image of a ship.

New works of restoration began in 1811 and ended in 1814. This is undoubtedly when the galleries in the northeast wing were divided up into cells, since the engineer in charge of the works had been told to keep in mind the fact that "in a prison it is necessary to have the greatest possible number of isolated rooms, leaving only a few in common for those persons who were not lucky enough to have a room all to themselves".

The prison had just begun to function well when the provisory government ordered all the prisoners to be freed.

In 1889 its status as a military building changed and a few years later it became a historical monument. Up until the end of the 19th century Dr. Peton, mayor of Saumur, had thought of transforming it into a museum. His dream became reality in 1906 when the city bought the château from the State for the incredibly low sum of 2500 francs and decided to begin restoration, sharing the costs with the Fine Arts Administration.

Large carved windows, the remains of great fireplaces, the stained-glass windows of the chapel, and glazed tiles under the earth fills were all brought to light. In particular a coin with the effigy of Louis XIV provided an approximate date for its transformation into a prison. It is however obvious that the 20th-century restoration, even though it was rigorously carried out, could not reproduce the sculptured decoration of the doors and windows and of the fireplaces with the magnificence they must have had in the 14th century.

In 1912 the first floor of the northeast wing, as well as the two towers which flank it, were allotted to the Municipal Museum, while the second floor is dedicated to the recently created Horse Museum.

Two suggestive pictures of the castle of Serrant.

SERRANT

In the 14th century the estate of Serrant belonged to the Le Brie family but the building that existed at the time was only later transformed into the castle we see today. Louis XI granted Pontus Le Brie permission to create a stronghold furnished with all kinds of defensive works on this spot.

Work began in 1546, under Charles Le Brie, who called in the famous architect Philibert Delorme, the designer of the wing of Chenonceaux so daringly suspended over the Cher.

Extremely symmetrical and stylistically unified, despite the fact that the construction work continued throughout the 16th and 17th centuries, the castle of Serrant clearly displays the influence of Renaissance art, like all the luxurious châteaux of the Loire from the time of Francis I on.

The new Renaissance modes (wide windows, pilasters, pediments, in which innovations of great elegance are inserted such as the domed roofs of the angle towers) harmonize perfectly with various archaic aspects

(the corner towers, the symmetrical layout, the presence of deep moats filled with water).

This is all quite evident in the magnificent facade. Note should be made first of all of the sense of color displayed by the use of shale and tuff, which create an elegant medley of brown and beige under the light line of the dormer windows and the dark slate roof. The double entrance is surmounted by a central body with windows and pilasters, on top of which is a sort of edicule with a triangular pediment. At the sides rows of windows let light into the rooms of the castle, which is now thought of in terms of comfort and beauty. On the top floor the powerful corner towers have a long balcony which completely surrounds them. They are roofed by two curious helmet-shaped domes which attempt to go beyond the older method of conical roofing. The upper hemisphere of each dome is surmounted by a lantern with a smaller analogous hemispherical roof. Stone bridges with arches supported by pilasters which terminate in pyramids lead

Following pages: The bedroom prepared for Napoleon I in 1808: above the fireplace, one can admire a bust of Empress Marie-Louise by Canova; The dining-room with Flemish tapestries on the walls; View of the library which boats over twenty thousand volumes.

over the wide moat at the side into the internal court.

While these structure were being built the owners of the castle - after the Le Brie family - were the duke of Montbazon Hercule de Roham (around 1596) and then, from 1636 on, the future count of Serrant, Guillaume de Bautru. A member of the parliament of Rouen when he was only 22, he was then intendent for Touraine and selector of the King's ambassadors and Court counselor. He is remembered for his polished wit, his salacious sense of satire and as a member of the Académie Française as well as for his activities as a diplomat and ambassador. One of his heirs was his granddaughter Margaret, whose husband, Marquis of Vaubrun and lieutenant general of the King's army, fell in the battle of Altenheim in 1675. In memory of her consort, Margaret had the chapel built on the extension of the right wing, on which Jules Hardouin-Mansart, who had already created the Gallery of Mirrors in the castle of Versailles, worked. A monumental tomb for the marquis was built inside, executed by the sculptor Coysevox on a design attributed to Charles Le Brun.

Thereafter the castle of Serrant belonged to an Irish nobleman, Antoine Walsh, and, after 1830, to the duke of Tremoille, to whose descendants it still belongs. Inside the château are magnificent furnishings, including tapestries of the Brussels manufacture in the library (with thousands of books) and two busts by Antonio Canova of the empress Marie Louise. Also worthy of note are the interior staircase, the dining room and the ground floor ceilings, decorated with coffering.

The chapel contains a polychrome relief with a Pietà in addition to the mausoleum of the marquis of Vaubrun.

The castle of Ussé, with its towers, seems to come out of a fairy tale.

USSÉ

The castle of Ussé, on the edge of the forest of Chinon, stands on an area that was already occupied in ancient times, as shown by the remains of tumulus tombs found nearby. The fort that was built here in the Middle Ages was square in plan with towers and belonged to the descendants of Guelduin de Saumur. In the XV century, when the royal seat was in Chinon, the castle belonged to Jeanne, daughter of the king and of Agnès Sorel, his mistress. When Jeanne married Antoine de Bueil, other towers and architectonic elements were added to the dwelling.

Jean III de Bueil, Jean IV who fell at Azincourt, and Jean V known as "the scourge of the English", courageous warrior in Normandy and Admiral of France, all lived at Ussé. The costruction of the castle, in its present forms, is due to the Bueil family. When Charles VII died, the Bueil family fell into disgrace: Jean V openly rebelled and sided with the League. In 1485 he ceded the castle to the house of Espinay, a noble Breton family which restructured the complex, as did the Valentinay family later.

The new Renaissance influences caused the new owners to tear down the wing which shut out the panorama towards the valley and to change the aspect of the façades. The interiors were also rebuilt and lower ceilings were installed. The Renaissance chapel in the park was built between 1520 and 1538 by Charles d'Espinay and his wife Lucrezia de Pons. Other works later involved the part of the castle which opened onto the court of honor and the side towards the valley where an Italianate pavilion overlooking the terraced gardens was realized.

A royal chamber was prepared inside the palace in case the king should come for a visit, although as chance would have it he never did. After the Revolution, which left the castle untouched, Ussé passed into the hands of the Duchess of Duras, Claire de Kersaint, who formed a literary circle here, then into the hands of the Countess of la Rochejacquelin and finally into those of the de Blacas family, to whose descendants it still belongs. The particularly elegant, fairy-tale-like appearance of this castle at the edge of a dark, mysterious forest seems to have influenced Charles Perrault's conception of the castle in his "Sleeping Beauty".

The castle, still flourishing and lived in, contains a great number of furnishings of great historical value: the royal chamber looks as it did in the XVIII century, while an antechamber contains a valuable XVI century Italian cabinet with intarsias.

The gallery on the ground floor has a collection of Flemish tapestries, while other tapestries from Brussels are exhibited in the drawing room. The collegiate in the park exhibits precious 16th century choir stalls as well as a delicate "Virgin and Child" by Luca della Robbia.

*The magnificent exterior of Valençay,
with its facade divided up by pillars.*

VALENÇAY

The name of Valençay probably derives from Valens, a Gallo-Roman owner of the estate which lies on a cliff overlooking the valley of the Nahon river. The original nucleus of buildings began to take form in the 3rd-4th centuries. A massive stone tower that was built between the 10th and the 11th centuries was the distant ancestor of the château we now see. The first real feudal castle was built at the beginning of the 13th century, perhaps by Gauthier, lord of Valençay. Inherited by the Chalon-Tonnerre family, it was restructured and enlarged. The so-called Guard-room, an immense vaulted room, dates to this period. It is situated under the court of honor, access to which is from the subterraneans of the castle through a corridor which probably connected the castle to the fortifications built to the north and west of the château. The other two sides were defended by the cliff and had no need of man-made defenses.

During the 15th century the seigniory of Valençay passed to the rich d'Etampes family who demolished the old manor around 1540 and commissioned a sumptuous new residence. It is not certain who the architect called in by Jacques d'Etampes was. The names of both Philibert de l'Orme and Jean de l'Espine have been made but no documentary proof in favor of one or the other exists.

Inspired by the neighboring castle of Chambord, Jacques d'Etampes had the fine entrance pavilion, a

sort of unusual tower, built. As at Chambord the three superposed orders of pilasters have sculptured capitals. With its crown of machicolations, emphasized by an elaborate frieze, this fine ensemble is one of the masterpieces of the Renaissance.

The angle towers and the main bodies of the building, highlighted by the fine Italian Gallery, also date to this period.

At the beginning of the 17th century Dominique d'Etampes continued the structure, adding the west wing of the palace - the one overlooking the park, and the one towards the east. The courtyard that opened on the valley was closed by an arcaded wall which connected the two wings of the building. The interiors were decorated by famous artists, including Jean Mosnier, who also worked in Cheverny and at the Palais du Luxembourg. The enthusiastic description of the château which Mademoiselle de Montpensier entrusted to her "Mémoires" after a sojourn at Valençay dates to 1653.

In the second half of the 17th century, trials, family altercations, complex problems of succession led to the decline of the d'Etampes family and the property passed into the hands of the Chaumont de la Millière family. It was then bought in 1766 by Charles Legendre de Villemorien, who undertook new works of restructuration. The east wing and the arcaded wall were demolished to open up the view over the city.

The chapel seen from the inner courtyard.

The great hall on the ground floor ▶
furnished in Empire style.

Around 1770 the west wing was also transformed with the construction of the elegant South Tower at the end towards the valley. De Villemorien also infused new life into the economy of the estate, creating a silk factory and a smithy and increasing the commercial activity.

His son, Comte de Luçay, who escaped the guillotine during the Revolution, ceded everything to Talleyrand in 1802 since he was no longer able to bear the burden of the costs involved in maintaining the property. "Monsieur de Talleyrand, I want you to buy a fine estate, I want you to receive the members of the Diplomatic Corps, esteemed foreigners, I want people to want to come to your house and that being invited constitutes a reward for the ambassadors of the sovereigns who will content me...". With these words Napoleon Bonaparte had his minister of Foreign Affairs acquire Valençay, which was officially turned over in May, 1803, for the notable sum of 1,600,000 francs, in the payment of which Napoleon himself contributed.

Chronicles relate that Talleyrand, accompanied by Catherine Worlée, took three days to visit the entire estate: the château with its more than a 100 rooms, the park of 150 hectares, the woods, the lands, the fields, the vineyards, 99 farms... for a total of 19,000 hectares, one of the largest feudal estates in France. As Napoleon had desired, for more than a quarter of a century the most important personalities of the time vied with each other to be received at Valençay by the great diplomat.

Laying the blame for the undertaking of the war in Spain on Talleyrand, Napoleon, who intended to use Valençay as he pleased, sentenced that it was to become the dwelling place of the Princes of Spain and their following for the circa six years they were in exile. When they arrived in May of 1808 the château proved insufficiently large to house their numerous following

A corner of the reception room.

The bathroom, furnished towards 1830.

who had to be lodged in the city, provoking considerable confusion.

To alleviate the gilded imprisonment of the princes, Napoleon ordered the unwilling Talleyrand, host-jailer, to construct the Theater near the Orangerie: a real theater in all senses, large enough to hold 150 spectators, with a stage as deep as the entire hall. The rich decoration of the interior is attributed to the Adam brothers, famous Scotch architects. It was inaugurated in 1810 and the most famous actors of the time appeared there. Some of the stage sets which were made in Paris have remained at the theater which will soon be in use once more.

It was also at the time of the sojourn of the Spanish princes that the park was completely surrounded by

The living room of the Spanish king Ferdinand VII, exiled to Valencay by Napoleon I from 1808 to 1814.

walls as a security measure. In 1806 Talleyrand had it turned into an English garden, setting up scenic routes and commissioning the architect Renard to build exotic constructions (the Turkish pavilion, the Cossack's house, the Egyptian temple, the Chinese bridge). The only building still extant is the one created for dances and other entertainment, which was later transformed into a hunting lodge. The imposing monumental staircase which joined the Duchess's garden to the vegetable garden has also disappeared. The park does however still contain the ice room which is as yet in working order.

On March 12, 1814, the Princes of Spain returned to their native land, and after the Congress of Vienna, the fall of the Empire and the return of the Bourbons, Talleyrand retired to Valençay with Dorothy, his nephew's wife and future Duchess de Dino, where he ordered considerable restructuration to be carried out

and cancelled all traces of the Spaniards. The château was reborn: sumptuous receivements and banquets marked by the culinary skill of the great Carême were given; the smithy, the saw mills, the silk factory were once more put into working order; sheep raising was augmented by crossbreeding with merinos from England.

Among the important persons who stayed in the château during the last years of Talleyrand's life were Duke Paul de Noailles, Princess de Lieven, Countess Tyskiewicz, Thiers, Balzac, Decazes, the Duke d'Orléans and, in 1834, George Sand.

Talleyrand died in Paris on May 17, 1838 and was buried in Valençay as he had asked. The château and the estate passed to Louis de Talleyrand-Périgord, named Duke of Valençay by Charles X.

Since 1980 the château has been the property of a Departmental Association which administers it.

The internal courtyard of the castle and a view of the famous gardens.

VILLANDRY

This elegant Renaissance château stands not far from the Loire and from ancient prehistoric menhirs. Originally a feudal stronghold stood on the spot where Philip Augustus king of France and Henry II Plantagenet king of England met on July 4, 1189. Their contrasts were arbitrated in the medieval tower that still stands in the southwest corner of the castle. Philip Augustus won out and his victory was then sanctioned by the peace of Azay.

A few centuries later the manor became the property of Jean le Breton, president of the Chamber of the Counts of Blois. Minister for Francis I, Jean was charged by the king with controlling the construction of the royal palaces of Fontainebleau and Chambord, since he was well versed in architecture. For himself, Jean le Breton (whose family originally came from Scotland) set out to build a palace which was just the opposite of the foreboding feudal castle.

The older structures, with the exception of the keep, were razed to the ground and in 1536 the construction of a new building with a U-shaped ground plan around a court of honor facing the valley of the Loire was begun. The two large L-shaped wings contain typically Renaissance elements borrowed from the palaces built at the beginning of the 16th century: large windows framed by pilasters with capitals in classic style, horizontal mouldings, large dormer windows decorated by superstructures with pediments and volutes.

The wide facades were enlivened with slight asymmetries (in the placing of the windows, the length and angle of the wings) and by the arched porticoes on two sides of the courtyard.

Partially surrounded by a moat with ground water, the castle was landscaped with large gardens laid out on three different levels.

Landscape gardening developed together with the Italian Renaissance and was conceived of as a pendant to the architecture. At the time, Italian style gardens were characterized by a geometric layout and a typically architectonic taste. In France this new fashion led to the creation of the "French garden", where the garden became larger, eliminating the perimetral walls and limiting the architectural structures in general. Convenient avenues ran along the flower beds where low hedge borders set off the decorative plants.

The gardens of Villandry are perfect examples of this concept - they are all large and are set on various terraces. Water is collected on the topmost level while

Four pictures of the famous gardens of Villandry.

a middle terrace lies on the same plane as the rooms on the ground floor of the castle (ornamental garden) and a lower level contains the ornamental vegetable gardens. The upper terrace, which extends to a wood of tall trees, consists of orchards criss-crossed by shady paths.

In line with this principle the entire park of Villandry is cut through by green galleries, placed above the neighboring gardens, so that they can be seen from above. The ornamental garden on the middle terrace in the part nearest the castle consists of the so-called "gardens of love". Here four large squares of box shrubs and flowers form motifs which symbolize the allegories of love. The square to the northwest, with its wounded hearts arranged according to the allegory of the ball, indicates passionate love, while the northeast square with fans, horns and billets-doux (at the center) represents adulterous love, dominated by yellow flowers. Tender love is symbolized in the southwest, with hearts separated by flames of love and by the masks worn for balls, while the last square on the southeast evokes tragic love with sword blades and the blood-red color of duels.

The southernmost part of the garden contains three large diamond-shaped beds enclosing the crosses of Languedoc, Malta and Béarn. Beyond the moat, lower down, the ornamental vegetable gardens lie between the castle and the edge of the town, with the Romanesque church in the corner. This part of the park is unique in the way in which the geometric designs of the large multicolored beds are created exclusively by vegetables and fruit plants. Long ago, in the 16th century, when the first botanic gardens were created, previously unknown plants were introduced from the Americas. Considered rarities, they were planted in the most prestigious gardens in Europe and were carefully tended so that they might adapt to the new climate. This was also what happened in Villandry and the original aspect of the nine large sections of the vegetable garden have been perfectly reconstructed thanks to the initiative of Dr. Joachim Carvallo, who replanted the old gardens in the early 1900s, basing himself on drawings by the landscape painter Androuet du Cerceau. Each vegetable garden creates geometrical motifs whose colors are provided by the leaves of cabbages, carrots, beets and lettuce. Apple and pear trees whose branches form lattices define and separate the beds. The gravel paths - like the center of the nine squares - are decorated with small fountains which were originally used for irrigation.

INDEX